Gilgamesh to Gierach

Gilgamesh to Gierach

Four Thousand Years of Fishing, Fish,
and Water Stories

by
James W. White

Foreword by Brian D. McLaren

Pen-and-ink illustrations by Ramona Lapsley
and Jim Vandermiller

WIPF & STOCK · Eugene, Oregon

GILGAMESH TO GIERACH
Four Thousand Years of Fishing, Fish, and Water Stories

Wipf & Stock
An Imprint of Wipf and Stock Publishers
199 W. 8th Ave., Suite 3
Eugene, OR 97401

www.wipfandstock.com

PAPERBACK ISBN: 979-8-3852-0568-4
HARDCOVER ISBN: 979-8-3852-0569-1
EBOOK ISBN: 979-8-3852-0570-7

VERSION NUMBER 08/01/24

Books, journal articles, poems, song lyrics, and Internet materials are fully cited in the footnotes of this book. Permissions to print have been obtained from Ramona Lapsley for use of her pen-and-ink fishing fly, from Jim Vandermiller for use of his pen-and-ink drawings, and for some stories. Permission is not required for the use of material in the public domain.

Although reasonable effort has been made to identify and contact copyright holders, in a few instances, this has not been possible, for obtaining permissions is like "looking for unicorns," as one researcher described the process. Still, if notified, the author stands ready to accommodate any copyright holder's requests in future editions.

Dedicated to

THE GOLDEN GHILLIES

Jamoca, Chauncey, and Gilda

and to

FRIENDS FISHED WITH, NAMELY

Kyle and Melissa Addington; Mike Alison; Jim Almond; Dick Anderson; Stuart Andrews; Wilson Arevalo; Xavier Arevalo-Surage; Lindy Baer; Bob Balls; Karen Barry; Rick Bayley; Jack Beal; Andy Blackman; Greg Blessing; Doug Brown; David Burnham; Jeff Campagna; Gary Carbaugh; Diane Carrerio; Miranda Cherry; Hal Chorpenning; Paul and Sarah Coleman; Alan Conger; Oliver Daley; Chad DeKaim; Marsha and Richard Duncan; Ron Dunn; Mel Emeigh; Mike and Vaughan Emerson; Donn Erickson; Ben and Ralph Everett; John Feek; Steve Ferguson; Joe Field; Guy Fredella; Georg Gehrung; Steve Gossage; Ron Granneman; John, Peter, and Vic Hallsten; Stan Harwood; Stuart Haskins; Dave Herber; Cy and Kass Holladay; Ronnie Jacobson; George Jamieson; Dave Johnson; Richard Johnson; Les Kitchen; Lawrence Kolz; Jeannie and Lyn Koneman; John Kurish; Blair and Bruce Kuster; Dave Lafrance; Eric Larsen; Jim Laughery; Lee and Neil Lehmkuhl; Becky and Dave Leinweber; Katie and Mike Lewis; Phil Lighty; Richard Limpert; Brad and Cheril Loper; Neil Luehring; John Maclin; Mark Mahler; Gordon McKay; Brian McLaren; Mark Henry Miller; Dan, Jim, Mike, and Sunny Moorhusen; Cat O'Grady; John Pierce; Reuben Rainey; Tom Rehling; Billy Rhue; Berkley Rich; Carl Roberts; Kent Saltonstall; Frank and Nick Sanborn; Bob Schluter; Sid Shelton; Rick Shick; Rick Steffens; John Stefonik; Anthony, Chloe, and Sophia Surage; Peter Terpennning; Christopher, Jon, and Peter Thomas; Rich Tosches; Bob and Polly Tucker; Jim Vandermiller; Greg Walters; Bruce and Jane Warren; David Weddle; Ben Weeks; Anita McCullough White; Becca White; Charlie White; Michelle White; Patti Limpert White; Lolise, Sevier, Yan Jun, and Yangtze White; Jim Williams; Russ Winger; Walt Winters; Hayley and Lauren Willson; Joe and Ken Wolf; Gary Young; Robert Younghanz; Brad Yuan ...

AND EVER SO MANY OTHERS.

Contents

Illustrations

Foreword

My maternal grandmother, Ivy Smith, was born in the 1890s. She was one of the sweetest, quietest, and most proper ladies you ever would have met if you were blessed enough to know her.

She could make a grape pie (a specialty of upstate New York) that would almost make you cry for its culinary transcendence. She even worked magic with white bread, leftover turkey, mayonnaise, and cranberry relish . . . I've never had a better sandwich than the ones she sent home with us when we came to visit for Thanksgiving.

I never once saw her yell or rush or be unkind to anyone. Behind her back, my grandfather said the same thing. "We've never raised our voices with each other," he would say. And I believed him.

Her hair was always perfectly curled and cut. She always had a tasteful necklace around her neck, along with tasteful earrings. I never saw her sweat.

I never saw my grandmother not in a dress or skirt either. Pants were men's clothing, she thought. Why would she ever lower her feminine dignity to that level?

There was one exception: She would wear a very modest swimsuit when we gathered for summer vacation at a cottage in the Finger Lakes. But she didn't wear it often because she didn't know how to swim. I have a vague memory of her floating in shallow water holding onto an air mattress, but, mostly, I remember her dangling her feet in the water on the end of the dock. Even that she would usually do in her dress or skirt, come to think of it.

Put that all together and you might be surprised that she was the person who taught me to fish. Her delight in fishing was so great that it was contagious, but I think, of all the grandkids, I was the only one who really caught a bad case of it from her. Grandpa would help her gingerly and discreetly step down from the dock into the back of an old rowboat. My brother or a cousin and I would be invited to climb down and sit in the front. I remember the bulky, bright-orange life jacket I had to wear because I was only four years old and, like my grandmother, couldn't swim.

Grandpa would have an old blue Maxwell House coffee can (same one, year after year) that he'd fill up with nightcrawlers from his garden. He would row us to her favorite spots, and, usually, he'd bait her hook. But if the bluegills and yellow perch were hungry and he was busy helping me untangle yet another knot, my grandmother would plunge her hand in the blue can and pull out a worm and bait the hook herself. Honestly, I still am amazed to think of it.

Fishing, especially fly fishing, is a lifelong sport. You can start when you're barely more than a toddler, and you can still be wetting a line when you're a hundred. I'm the age now that my grandmother was when we used to fish together, and I'd be really happy if my last day on earth involved a rod, some water, some fish, and one of my children's children or even their grandchildren.

My friend Jim White has about 80 years of fishing under his belt, and he's still going strong. In this lovely book, he tells us that fishing, especially fly fishing, is the most literary of sports. And his career proves it with many delightful articles and books to his credit on the subject.

This, his newest book, may well be the most comprehensive literary survey of fishing literature ever written—at least in terms of the amount of history it covers and the genres it takes into account. It may, in fact, be the *only* comprehensive survey of fishing literature ever written, which would, I suppose, render the book the greatest of its genre. Consider yourself fortunate to have found it! As you'll soon see, it's a pleasure to read and takes you on a journey around the world and across history.

Jim starts with *The Epic of Gilgamesh* and jumps from fish tale to fish tale until you find yourself washed up on the shores of the present. Yes, he cheats a bit and includes some whale tales. But Jim is such a master storyteller of his own fishing experiences and a master reteller of the experiences of others that the only people who will complain about including whales would be the same kind of humorless, literalist, anti-literary scoundrels who would complain about an angler enhancing the truth about the number or size of his catch.

Those of us who know the physical, social, psychological, and spiritual joys of fishing (and perhaps the occasional gastronomic joys too) also know that the pleasures of fishing involve a wide range of other pleasures . . . joke telling; story telling; bald-faced lying; uproarious laughing; pranks, including ones that backfire; companionship; food and drink, sometimes including alcoholic spirits—not to mention the enjoyment of nature and physical exercise, and, quite often, sincere spiritual rumination and contemplative insight.

If you put all these pleasures together, fishing is such an amazing endeavor that it's a wonder many of us ever do anything else. It is not a wonder, however, that if we can't be fishing, many of us would, at least, like to be reading about fishing, and, for that, we once again have Jim White to thank. Not only does Jim compile great fishing stories from the canons of literature, but he serves us up some great fishing poetry, some great cinematic fishing moments, and some not-too-shabby fishing jokes too.

Reading this book isn't quite as amazing as landing a 14-inch greenback cutthroat or watching a silver tarpon leap six feet into the air, trying to dislodge your fly from his upper lip. But if you love fishing—or if you're trying to understand why someone you love loves fishing so darn much—this book is just what you need.

I have to tell you, having just finished it, I have the biggest smile on my face.

Brian D. McLaren
Marco Island, Florida

Preface

Something there is in us that simply loves a story, that wants it told. From childhood's "Tell me a story and then I'll go to bed" to the attention given to the recitation of a friend's obituary, we listen to, create, tell, and retell stories. So it has been since time immemorial. We are born in a story, live one out, and die in one. Along the way, we are entertained, instructed, and inspired by various tellings and readings. The introduction to one collection of the *Grimms' Fairy Tales*—which tales include some stories involving fishing, fish, and water ever magic—offers an explanation for the enduring value of stories of all kinds. The translator, who wrote the introduction, says,

> Wherever tales still exist they continue to live in such a way that nobody ponders whether they are good or bad, poetic or crude. People know them and love them because they have simply absorbed them in a habitual way. And they take pleasure in them without having any reason. This is exactly why the custom of storytelling is so marvelous. And it is just what this poetic art has in common with everything eternal.[1]

Those words are true for the brothers' tales and for most stories, especially those selected for recapping in this collection. I will be lifting up tales that appeal to readers generally and, most specifically, to storytellers, fly-fishing anglers, and lovers of good literature. The hope is that these accounts of old as well as of this current age will enrich the reader's own story.

Tales involving anglers, fish, and water have been with us a long time—at least from 2100 B.C.E. with *The Epic of Gilgamesh*. And new tales appear in the third millennium C.E. courtesy of, among others, John Gierach, a fly-fishing author. Not only do the names Gilgamesh and Gierach span millennia, but they provide congenial alliterative framing for this collection. In

1. Jack Zipes, translator of the introduction to Jacob and Wilhelm Grimm's *The Original Folk and Fairy Tales of the Brothers Grimm: The Complete First Edition* (Princeton, NJ: Princeton University, 2016). This author, afflicted by macular degeneration, *heard* the book on BARD (Braille and Audio Reading Downloads, a resource provided for the visually impaired by the U.S. Library of Congress). As an audible book, it does not have page numbers for citation.

between Gilgamesh and Gierach is a vast literary corpus—legendary, biblical, novelistic, poetic, archaic, contemporary, even fantasy-driven. In these pages, I identify over 300 stories and other works and retell a few of them in full, most of them in summary or paraphrase. Some get only a few lines but always enough, it is hoped, to communicate the spirit of the pieces. In addition, for the scholarly inclined, sources are provided in both the footnotes and the bibliography.

An all-inclusive anthology of fishing tales, most assuredly, would be massive. Holly Morris, writing in *The New York Times* about fishing literature, says, "The English language boasts more than 5,000 books on fishing. Fishing, particularly fly fishing, is without doubt our most literary sport."[2] One collection among the thousands is *The Gigantic Book of Fishing Stories*, edited by Nick Lyons. Most of the books mentioned by Morris were spawned in the 20th century, and most are generally excellent, basically true, and North American in origin and coverage.

This book briefly reviews many such tales. The stories, using the word loosely, in this new collection, however, are different. They are centuries deeper, more imaginative, and of broader literary and geographical compass. They include legends, fables, myths, bible tales, poems, songs, and even jokes. They have been fun to find and to present even if in abbreviated fashion. My desire is that readers will be drawn in by what they discover here and then will seek the complete accounts of, say, "The Salmon of Knowledge" or Thomas McGuane's *The Longest Silence*. In complete or condensed form, these tales, poems, songs, and more may be enjoyed for pure pleasure by the fireside, but some also will offer information and insights.

Necessarily, there are limits to what is under consideration here.

First of all, consider *fishing*. Fishing is an enormously broad subject, done in myriad ways, by bait casting, lure and spinner retrieving, harpooning, downrigger trolling, gill netting, dynamiting (!), and ocean long-lining. If these broader ways of angling are touched on in these pages, it will be but lightly, but they do appear, as in *Arabian Nights* and *Moby Dick*. That said, the focus in these pages mostly is on fly fishing as it has been done through the centuries in sundry locales from Yellow River, China, to Yellowstone Park, USA.

Secondly, the stories are about *fish*, especially salmonoid and char trout. Occasionally, a story will involve a warm-water species, such as bass, pike, or crappie. Saltwater species mentioned could be bonefish, permit, sharks, whales (technically mammals), and mermaids(!). The number of

2. Holly Morris, "Fumbling After Grace: Fishing and Writing," *New York Times*. June 8, 1997. In my personal library alone, there are over 150 angling and angling-related books.

water creatures—minnows to marlin to monsters—is enormous. Only a few are considered in this collection.

Thirdly, the stories are about *water*, which could take us planet-wide and deep. The pre-Socratic philosopher Heraclitus understood water as the foundational element of the world, taking precedence over earth, wind, and fire. In this book, waters wide (oceans and seas) are considered but freshwaters—whether they be spring creeks or famous rivers—are the usual medium. Even so, diverse wider waters appear in the tales: the Sea of Galilee, the Newfoundland Banks, the vast Pacific, a Caribbean estuary, even an Oklahoma farm pond. Ian Bradley of St. Andrews University, Scotland, found water to be a frequent metaphor for heaven, life, encounters with God, and journeys to the next world.[3] That may be why, in part, men and women are found "standing in a river waving a stick," as author John Gierach puts it.[4]

Ever-inside the fishing, fish, and water tales of this book are *people*, fictitious or actual, the men and women who go down to the crawdad hole—or watery depths—such as Odysseus, Celtic monks, Dame Juliana Berners, Captain Nemo, Roderick Haig-Brown, and dozens of others. The accounts regularly tell us something about the storytellers themselves: Roman poet Martial, Charles Cotton, Henry David Thoreau, Garrison Keillor, or Norman Maclean, for example. Female characters, real or imagined, are in these pages: Izaak Walton's milkmaids, Yeat's glimmering girl, Anglican angler Laurie on her white camel, and mystery author Mary Roberts Rinehart, to name a few.

From time to time, I interject a thought of my own or share a personal angling experience.

There are myriad ways that the literature included in this book might be classified—by date of composition, author of tales, countries and waters discussed. In this book, I have organized the tales by *type of literature*, having identified 12 genres in which are considered fishing (especially fly fishing), fish species (mythical to edible, focusing on trout), waters wide (Tigris River to Canadian lakes), and sundry authors and actors (Ovid to David James Duncan's Gus Orviston) as they attend to "the contemplative man's recreation," as Izaak Walton in *The Compleat Angler* speaks of the sport.

3. Ian C. Bradley, *Water: A Spiritual History* (New York: Bloomsbury Publishing, 2012).

4. John Gierach, *Standing in a River Waving a Stick* (New York: Simon and Schuster, 1999).

Acknowledgments

Greater in number than the number of fish species I know—Alligator gar to fish-tank Zebras—are the number of people who have helped this octogenarian put fish tales on paper—from a fishing friend named Adam to a fishing guide called Zorba.

Top of the list must be Pattigirl, wife and woman extraordinaire, indefatigable and omnicompetent. How often she has rescued me from despair in writing, patiently fixing stories and inviting me to a restorative table, Spanish rioja included!

I also would have readers give it up especially for Wendy Demandante, editor extraordinaire, who has made this a better book by source findings, text fixing, and skilled wordsmithing. She got it to the finish line whole, much-the-more readable. Reuben Rainey, Jim Williams, and Lauren Willson have read the entire manuscript and graciously offered fixes, improvements, and deletions.

Whimsical pen-and-ink illustrations accompany several tales in this book. They were drawn by my good friend and fellow angler Jim Vandermiller. I'm grateful for his sketches that visually spice up the text of this book. The icon fly, which separates sections in the chapters, was drawn by Manitou Springs artist Ramona Lapsley.

In the past, I have dedicated books to my now-deceased parents, daughters Cheril and Melissa, granddaughters Hayley and Lauren Willson, my friend Bruce Kuster with whom I have fished more than 60 years, and Patti. Physically, electronically, and in spirit, all have been with me these years of collection and composition. What a blessing, they!

My gratitude also extends to many, many others. Feeding me cultural stories for inclusion here has been librarian Kathy Beck and Colorado College historian Carol Neel. Not to forget generous leads, materials, and corrections offered by Rick Bayley, Peter Burford, Ed Elkins, Karol Finch, Henry Hughes, Alyce Morgan, Reuben Rainey, Greg Walters, and David Weddle.

Of sustaining personal assistance have been Andy Kort, Gordon McKay, Kelli Scarborough, Pat Steffens, Jean Tidball, and Ani Rose Whaleswan.

They read books, magazines, and papers that my macular-degenerative eyes could not decipher. In addition, I have been able to listen to books by BARD—Braille and Audio Reading Downloads—a service provided by the National Library Service for the Blind and Print Disabled. All have helped me keep illiteracy at bay.

Typing on the manuscript has been done by Hannah Hokanson, Monica Weindling, and Patti. Computer support has come via Carolyn Dickerson, Lynn Holladay, Robbie Limpert, Sid Shelton, Paul Schwotzer, and Robin Walters.

When computer-screen hours and straining have been too much, Greg Walters, Anthony Surage, John Kurish, Neil Luehring, Mark Mahler, Jon Thomas, and others have whisked me away to trout waters. As they tied on flies, they patiently listened to the latest report on the book.

For each and all, my gratitude is deep and wide. Thank you, sincerely.

Chapter 1

Cultural Tales

Microscopic traces of wood ash, examined by carbon dating, suggest controlled use of fire by *Homo erectus*, beginning roughly one million years ago. We can well imagine primitive men, women, and children gathering 'round the fire pit. There, they certainly heard stories, since human language had developed a million years earlier.

Now, let a few hundred thousand years go by, our species has spread to the four corners of the planet, and billions of campfires have been sat around. Old stories were told and adapted. New ones were created, perhaps revealed, each suited to different places, times, people, and cultures. Insofar as our ancestors lived near, on, or by water—as water is required for survival—they naturally spun stories related to that life-giving element. Some stories explained things. Some simply entertained. All involved beings, real or imaginary, acting and interacting, igniting the imagination of fireside listeners, ever shaping their world. Some tales survived to come down to us. The reason that the ancient tales lasted is not because they never were true but because they always are true—as German novelist Thomas Mann contended about myths generally.[1]

So, cultural folktales, legends, and myths are the first genre of fishing-fish-water stories for consideration in this book. Below is an incomplete listing of such poems and tales presented by country of origin, a few of which are considered in the pages to follow.[2]

1. Exactly where Mann said or wrote this, I am not sure. I only know that, in 1960, Yale Divinity School Professor of Old Testament Studies B. Davie Napier quoted Mann to the effect that Cain's slaying of his brother Abel, for instance, is myth, something that never happened but is ever-occurring—never *was* but always *is* the truth.

2. Margaret Read MacDonald and Brian W. Sturm's *The Storyteller's Sourcebook* provides many other tales.

Alaska	"Sedna"
Canada	"How the Salmon Came to the Squamish"
England	"The Fish and the Ring"
	"The Lost Fisherman"
Greece	"Arion and the Dolphin"
	"The Odyssey"
Iceland	"Marmadill Who Laughed Three Times"
	"The Seal's Skin"
India	"The Golden Fish"
Iraq	"The Epic of Gilgamesh"
Ireland	"The Salmon of Knowledge"
Japan	"Urashima Tarō"
North America	"Bloodclot and the Sucker Fish"
	"The Fisherman and the Bear"
Scotland	"The Selkie Bride"
West Africa	"Anansi's Fishing Expedition"

These stories are fun to read, rich in meaning, and culturally distinct—though some do cross topographical boundaries. Let me share a few, enough for readers to get a feel for this category of tales.

What is likely the oldest piece of literature in the West is *The Epic of Gilgamesh*,[3] a Sumerian-Akkadian poem, dating from the third millennium B.C.E. This is not a fishing story per se, but, certainly, the story is watery and focuses on "the man who saw the deep," making Gilgamesh's *Epic* an excellent starting tale for this book.

The Epic of Gilgamesh is a 1,200-verse poem about Gilgamesh, King of Uruk, a city-state located in Lower Mesopotamia. The poem dates from around 2100 B.C.E. Tradition has it that Gilgamesh was two-thirds god and one-third human although he may have been a 100-percent-human historical figure. For centuries, his life story was carried—and embellished—by oral tradition but, eventually, was recorded on clay tablets using a complex

3. Over the years, *The Epic of Gilgamesh* has had several translations and iterations. N. K. Sandars edited a version in the 1970s that was updated with new scholarly shaping for its 2014 and 2021 editions. On BARD, I listened to it and, later, obtained a printed copy, it being Sandars, *The Epic of Gilgamesh*. Only the Egyptian *Book of the Dead*, made up of ancient funeral *prayers*, is older than the *story* of Gilgamesh.

cuneiform (wedge-shaped) script in the middle of the second millennium. In such form, the poem circulated widely in the Levant, best preserved by the Assyrians in ancient Nineveh. By about 750 B.C.E., however, all tablets referencing the Gilgamesh story seem to have been lost.

It wasn't until the archaeological flurry of the 19th century that Nineveh (near today's Mosul, Iraq) was thoroughly excavated. In 1853, partial tablets containing this ancient story were unearthed and sent to the British Museum to be deciphered. In subsequent diggings, additional fragments were discovered, adding to the text.

The epic poem says that Gilgamesh was "the man who saw the deep." I take that line to mean both the depth of water *and* the depth of life's meaning. His story is that of a tragic hero. In the poem, we learn that Gilgamesh, "the civilized man," fought with Enkidu, "the wild man" of the hills who ate grass and ran like a gazelle. (Wild Enkidu had been tamed by a prostitute, who also introduced him to beer and bread.) After their fight, Gilgamesh and Enkidu became the best of friends, perhaps lovers. Together, they went on many adventures, especially to the cedar forests of Lebanon. There, they slayed the monster Humbaba. On one occasion, they fought with lions.[4] They also had to elude the clutches of the goddess Ishtar, who lived by the mouth of the Tigris River and wanted to marry Gilgamesh. Rejected, she sent a bull to slay the two, but they kill it, and, then, Ishtar kills Enkidu.

Gilgamesh, despondent at the death of his best friend, uses the time of mourning to consider his own mortality. His search for eternal life leads him to distant mountains—the mountains of the rising and setting sun. Via a tunnel, he goes through the mountains to a watery shore. There, Siduri, the maker of wine, directs him to the ferryman Urshanabi on the Sea of Death,[5] who takes Gilgamesh over the water to meet Utnapishtim ("the faraway") and his wife. The couple are the only ones on earth to escape drowning in a great flood. They survived by boarding an ark along with many animals. After the flood, they were given eternal life. Gilgamesh asks Utnapishtim to help him escape death, but the old man explains that he cannot do so. His wife, though, helps by directing Gilgamesh to go to the deepest part of the sea, where the Plant of Eternal Youth will be found. We read,

> When Gilgamesh heard this he opened the sluices so the sweet-water current might carry him out to the deepest channel; he tied heavy stones to his feet and they dragged him to the water-bed. There he saw the plant growing; although it pricked him he

4. Lions appear with Gilgamesh in iconography.

5. Cf. Charon, the ferryman in Greek mythology who takes shades of the dead across the River Styx to Hades.

took it in his hands; then he cut the heavy stones from his feet,
and then the sea carried him and threw him on the shore.[6]

King Gilgamesh in the Depths

(Though the ancient text does not say it, Gilgamesh, I posit, went down and back up with catchable fish looking on!) Back on terra firma, he and Urshanabi head for Uruk. En route, a serpent from the netherworld crawls out of a well and steals the treasured plant forever.[7]

6. Sandars, *Epic of Gilgamesh*, 58.

7. Much of the above sounds similar to the later biblical story of Noah and the ark and also that of Adam, Eve, and the serpent in the Garden of Eden. Flood stories are told worldwide, China to Africa and beyond, the Roman poet Ovid having one in *Metamorphoses*.

Immortality lost, Gilgamesh then builds a great wall around the city, his compensatory memorial. Although most of the story is mythic, remnants of the wall of Uruk have been excavated and continue to be uncovered. Still, more than by a wall, Gilgamesh achieved his true immortality through the poem that tells his story.

Thus, in brief, we have *The Epic of Gilgamesh*, the man who saw the deep.

Millennia later, men and women fishing have found considerable meaning when "walking beside still waters" (Psalm 23) or beside waters flowing freely, often deep. Anthropologist and natural-science writer Loren Eiseley says it well, "If there is any magic on this planet, it is contained in water."[8]

Before the tablets containing *The Epic of Gilgamesh* were discovered in 1853, the oldest literature known in the West was Homer's *The Iliad* and *The Odyssey*, epic poems revered and quoted for millennia. *The Iliad* is the story of the Greek-Trojan War (1194–1184 B.C.E.) while *The Odyssey* takes up after Troy's defeat. After the war, the warrior Odysseus sets sail for his home in Ithaca, where his wife Penelope waits for him. However, the god Poseidon, who favored the defeated Trojans, has it in for Odysseus and blows him and his men around the Aegean Sea for years—10, as the story goes. At one point, after escaping past the island of the Sirens, the Greeks must navigate between two female monsters: Charybdis, a whirlpool who swallows up ships only to spit them out, and Scylla with six heads, which allow her to efficiently eat sailors. Here is what Odysseus says happened:

> My crew turned pale as we gazed at her, fearing destruction, but even as we did so Scylla seized six of my strongest and ablest men from the deck. As I looked along the swift ship towards my friends, I saw their arms and legs dangling above me. In anguish they cried my name aloud one last time, then each of Scylla's heads dragged a man writhing towards the rock, as a fisherman on a jutting crag casts his bait to lure small fish, lowers an ox-horn on a long pole into the sea, and, catching a fish, flings it ashore. There at the entrance to her cave she devoured them, as they shrieked and reached out their hands to me in their last dreadful

8. Eiseley, *Immense Journey*, 15.

throes. It was the most pitiable sight of all I saw exploring the pathways of the sea.[9]

Odysseus Between the Devil and the Deep Blue Sea

Book 12 of *The Odyssey* certainly suggests that Homer understood rod angling, for, in addition to the above excerpt but found in another translation of that same section, Homer states that Odysseus saw . . .

A man surfcasting on a point of rock
For bass and mackerel,
Whipping his long rod
To drop sinker and the bait far out,
Will hook a fish
And rip it from the surface
To dangle, wriggling through the air.[10]

9. Homer, *Odyssey* (trans. Klein), bk 12, lines 201–59.

10. Homer, *Odyssey* (trans. Fitzgerald), bk 12, lines 300–305.

One cannot find a clearer fishing-by-bait-casting tale earlier than this of the 13th century B.C.E. It is easy to imagine that the man described caught some of those bass and mackerel.

Now, a third cultural tale, decidedly fishy, though about a mammal, is a story told as true by ancient Greek historian Herodotus. His history of the Greco-Persian Wars, 497–449 B.C.E., is thought to be reasonably accurate. Interspersed with his credible history are folk legends, such as "Arion and the Dolphin."

The story is that Arion was a celebrated poet, singer, and musician from Lesbos who pleased Periander, the tyrant (king) of Corinth. Periander sent Arion to Tarentum, Italy, to compete in a music contest. Arion won the competition by singing and playing his kithara, a type of lyre. His prize was a chest of gold, silver, pearls, and other gems. To return home to Corinth, Arion engaged a ship, captain, and crew. The crew, however, sought to murder Arion for his winnings. He begged permission to sing one last song. After the last verse, Arion jumped into the sea, kithara on his back, risking drowning. Here is a verse from the poem about Arion's marvelous rescue:

> But the dolphin came and saved him.
> He rode it on the rolling waves.
> They crossed the sea to Corinth,
> The dolphin and the bard.

Unfortunately, once the dolphin landed him, the creature died. In its honor, a great statue was erected with a base hollowed out, leaving enough space to shelter a man.

As the story goes, sometime thereafter, the ship of the traitorous captain and crew was blown into the Corinth port. Asked about Arion, the captain explained to King Periander that his passenger, in a terrible storm, had been blown overboard and drowned, the treasure chest also lost. Knowing otherwise, Periander searched the vessel, found the treasure chest hidden on board (half of its contents belonged to him as king), and then brought Arion out of his hiding place in the base of the dolphin statue. The captain and crew were then crucified on the site. As Herodotus tells it, eventually, the Greek gods put the dolphin in the heavenly zodiac as the constellation Delphinium, so that, to this day, it can be seen between Sagittarius and Aquarius, ever to guide mariners.

Thus, history was told in the ancient world. If the father of history, Herodotus, handed down nonhistorical legends, Pliny the Elder in Rome

(23–79 C.E.) also got some things wrong. In his encyclopedic book *The Natural History*, he reports on "monsters in the sea," of which we are told:

> The largest number of animals and those of the largest size are in the Indian sea, among them whales covering three acres each, and sharks *100* ells long [an ell being *45* inches]: In fact in those regions lobsters grow to *6* ft. long, and also eels in the river Ganges to *300* ft. The monsters in the sea are mostly to be seen about the solstices.[11]

By contemporary aquatic investigation, we now know the biggest eels in the world seldom reach more than 10 feet. Pliny, then, may have told fish tales as fish tales are usually understood—with generous exaggeration.

Less exaggerated are the findings of Aristotle (364–322 B.C.E.) to be considered more fully in Chapter 7. Judging by his *History of Animals*, which includes consideration of fish species, Aristotle could be considered the world's first ichthyologist. For millennia, he was thought to have got fish taxonomy right. He did not, however, tell fish stories qua fish stories or legends we might include in this chapter.

What will fit is an account from Indian culture as told by Herman Melville in *Moby Dick*. He says that the Hindu god Vishnu was given the task of retrieving sacred Vedas from the bottom of the ocean. About this, Melville writes,

> Vishnu became incarnate in a whale, and sounding down in him to the uttermost depths, rescued the sacred volumes. Was not this Vishnu a whaleman, then? Even as a man who rides a horse is called a horseman?[12]

Indeed, Vishnu was a whaleman—or deep-sea diver or bottom-trawling fisherman. So, "from the depths," the sacred texts surfaced.

Now we move farther west for a mythical tale about fish—or semi-fish. This story comes from the Scottish Isles. It's about a selkie or shape-shifting creature, half-human and half-seal.[13] The story goes like this (my paraphrasing): Once upon a time [as these stories ought to begin], there was a fisherman.

11. Pliny the Elder, *Natural History*, bk 9, p. 167.

12. Melville, *Moby Dick* (1980), 319.

13. In Norse and Celtic mythology, selkies or selkie-folk, meaning "seal folk," are mythological beings capable of therianthropy, the ability to change from animal to human form.

One day, coming home, walking along the beach, he came upon selkie-folk, dancing on the shore. For the dancing, they had shed their skins. Passing by, the fisherman spotted a seal skin on a shore rock, picked it up, and carried it home. There, he hid it in a fireplace crevice.

Soon thereafter, a beautiful girl knocked on his cottage door, asking about the skin. Well, the two fell in love, were married, and had children. Often, though, the woman was found looking wistfully out to sea.

After many years, one of their children found the seal skin hidden in the chimney and gave it to his mother. She carried it down to the seashore, put it on, and swam away.

Often thereafter, a certain grey seal would swim alongside the fisherman's boat and bark atop a bay rock as the children walked the shoreline. It was said that this seal always had a tear in her eye.[14]

This story has many variations from Ireland to Norway—even to the Arctic. An Icelandic version has a mer*man* (not a maid), called a marbendill in their tongue, come ashore and leave the Icelanders their distinctive breed of cattle, which are blue-gray as are sea cows!

From Ireland comes yet another great legend of this genre. This Irish legend is called "The Salmon of Knowledge" or, in full, "Fionn MacCumhaill and the Salmon of Knowledge." Here is my summary retelling of the tale: At the biblical time of the great deluge, God allowed one worthy man, Fintan, to escape by turning him into a salmon. That salmon swam up the Boyne River in Ireland to where there was a deep pool. Nine hazel trees hung above the pool, each bearing a hazelnut, which nuts, when taken together, contained all the knowledge of the world. When the trees' nuts matured, they fell into the pool. The salmon swallowed them. Thus, he became the Salmon of Knowledge.

In time, when Earth was repopulated, people sought to catch Fintan, the most knowledgeable and elusive salmon. Finally, after seven years angling, one man did, Druid poet and fisherman Finegas. He hooked the mystical fish and, after an exhausting fight, landed it. Finegas was overjoyed, for he knew that, in eating the fish, he would be not only the wisest druid in Ireland but, also, the wisest man in the entire world. Finegas' apprentice, Fionn, placed the salmon on a spit over a fire and started to cook the fish. Exhausted by his great struggle to land the salmon, Finegas instructed the young man to tend the fire while the fisherman napped. When the salmon finished cooking, the lad called Finegas to come for his meal. In taking the cooked salmon off the fire, however, some burning fat from it splashed on

14. "The Selkie Bride," https:www.weingartdesign.com/TMaS/stories/tmas1-selkiebride.html.

Finn's hand. The youngster merely stuck his thumb into his mouth, as one does with such a burn. Soon, Finegas arrived with his eating salver but immediately recognized that there was something different about his young pupil. He demanded to know whether Fionn had eaten any of the fish. The boy denied this, but Finegas knew otherwise and now knew it was not his destiny to receive the great wisdom from the salmon. Instead, it was to be the destiny of Fionn MacCumhaill (usually anglicized to "Finn McCool") to become the greatest king of Ireland and "greatest of all men."[15]

Skipping across the Atlantic to North America and across this continent to the Pacific Northwest, we pick up a Native American tale of how the salmon came to the Squamish tribe, as follows: Long, long ago, they say, their ancestors living inland and far up the river were often starving. One day, though, four good brothers came to their village and heard of their plight. The brothers then consulted Snookum the Sun about what to do. Snookum instructed them to go downriver, west, to the ocean. This they all did and, after many days paddling, came to an island where the Salmon People dwelt. Arriving there, the Squamish presented gifts, and, in anticipation of their guests' arrival, the Salmon Chief sent four of his young people into the water, where they became fish. The fish then swam into the tribe's traps and were retrieved and roasted for a feast. However, the feast came with the instruction to throw the bones in the water, and, when the bones were so cast, the young people miraculously came back to life. The visiting brothers ask the chief of the Salmon People if he would send fish up the river to the Squamish in the future.

> "I will do as you request," replied the Salmon Chief, "on one condition: they must throw all the bones back into the water as you have seen us do. If they will be careful with the bones, my people can return to us again after they visit you."
>
> "We promise," said the four brothers.
>
> "We promise," said all the Squamish people.
>
> Then they made preparations to return to their home across the water, toward the rising sun. As they were leaving, the Salmon Chief said, "I will send Spring Salmon to you first in the season. After them I will send the Sockeye, then the Coho, then the Dog-Salmon, and last of all the Humpback."
>
> Ever since that time, long ago, different kinds of salmon, in that order, have come to the Squamish waters, to the sea, into the straits, and into the streams. And in the days of old, before

15. "Finn MacCumhaill."

the coming of the white people, the Indians were always very careful to throw the bones of the salmon back into the water.[16]

For our next cultural tale, let us cross the Pacific for a condensed (by me) story of Japan's Urashima Tarō. Urashima Tarō, a young fisherman, comes across some boys tormenting a tortoise. He rescues the tortoise and returns it to the sea.[17] The next day, when he is out fishing on the Sea of Japan, the grateful tortoise comes aboard Urashima's boat and bids him ride on its back to the palace of Rin Chin, the sea king, at the bottom of the ocean. He is ushered into the palace by many fish. There, Urashima meets a beautiful princess, the sea king's daughter, who seems to be the transfigured tortoise. The two marry and are set to live forever. After a time, though, Urashima remembers his elderly father and mother and asks that he might return home to care for them. His wife agrees and swims him back, giving him a special lacquered box, which he is told never to open.

On land again, Urashima finds he has been gone 300 years, not just a few days! He knows no one, and no one knows him. Urashima then wants to go back to his princess and the sea king's familiar palace, but he can't. In desperation, he disobeys his wife's instructions and opens the lacquered box. Out comes a deadly spirit which causes Urashima Tarō to age quickly and then die alone on the spot.[18]

The Urashima Tarō story, like many other fables, conveys lessons for the hearer. The concluding moral message in the Urashima legend is, "Little children, never be disobedient to those who are wiser than you, for disobedience was the beginning of all the miseries and sorrows of life."[19] The story also conveys a message to be kind—especially to animals.

The North Atlantic and Pacific stories recounted above, like other cultural tales, are often etiological—telling where, when, or how things came to be—but, often, stories simply function to fire a reader's imagination about life in the mysterious watery depths, and that is good enough.

16. "Why the Salmon Come to the Squamish Waters," in "Native American Legends."

17. Technically, it must be a turtle, since tortoises are land animals.

18. "Story of Urashima Tarō." The website's original source is Y. T. Ozaki, *Japanese Fairy Tales*. Another good retelling is in Chiyino Sugimoto's *Picture Tales From the Japanese*.

19. "Story of Urashima Tarō."

Chapter 2

Fables

Closely related to cultural tales, legends, and myths are fables. As ancient as some of the previous tales that we have considered, most of the following fables are attributable to an author, and most have a moral lesson. Here are some fables that included references to fishing, fish, or water:

Aesop's Fables (sixth to fifth century B.C.E.)

- "The Fisherman and the Little Fish"
- "The Great and the Little Fishes"
- "The Monkey and the Dolphin"
- "The Monkey and the Fishermen"

The Arabian Nights or *The Thousand and One Nights* (ninth century C.E. ff.)

- "The Fisherman and the Bottle"
- "The Voyage of Sinbad the Sailor"

Robert Dodsley, "The Trout and the Gudgeon" (18th-century England)

Grimms' Fairy Tales (1812)

- "The Fisherman and His Wife"
- "The Lambkin and the Little Fish"

Arthur Ransome, *Old Peter's Russian Tales* (20th-century England)

- "Fish in the Forest"
- "The Golden Fish"
- "The Great Pike and the Little Fish"

From online sources:

- "The Bittern and the Mussel" (China)
- "The Heron and the Crab" (India)
- "The Two Fishermen and the Three Fishes" (Iran)

We begin with *Aesop's Fables,* attributed to Aesop of Athens, Greece. He was a slave and storyteller in the sixth and fifth centuries B.C.E. His fables may have been drawn from other traditions, such as Indian ones, and they most certainly were retold in Roman culture. About the fables, the first-century writer Apollonius of Tyana says,

> Like those who dine well off the plainest dishes, [Aesop] made use of humble incidents to teach great truths, and after serving up a story he adds to it the advice to do a thing or not to do it. Then, too, he was really more attached to truth than the poets are; for the latter do violence to their own stories in order to make them probable; but he by announcing a story which everyone knows not to be true, told the truth by the very fact that he did not claim to be relating real events.[1]

Apollonius has it right about Aesop's work, and it is true about other fable-tellers as well. We begin with Aesop's "The Monkey and the Fishermen":

> A Monkey was sitting up in a high tree, when, seeing some Fishermen laying their nets in the river, he watched what they were doing. The Men had no sooner set their nets, and retired a short distance to their dinner, than the Monkey came down from the tree, thinking that he would try his hand at the same sport. But in attempting to lay the nets he got so entangled in them, that being well-nigh choked, he was forced to exclaim: "This serves me right; for what business had I, who know nothing of fishing, to meddle with such tackle as this?"[2]

An equally excellent fish-and-water Aesop fable is "The Monkey and the Dolphin," moral included. Here it is:

> A sailor, bound on a long voyage, took with him a Monkey to amuse him while on shipboard. As he sailed off the coast of Greece, a violent tempest arose in which the ship was wrecked and he, his Monkey, and all the crew were obliged to swim for their lives. A Dolphin saw the Monkey contending with the waves, and supposing him to be a man (whom he is always said to befriend), came and placed himself under him, to convey him on his back in safety to the shore. When the Dolphin arrived with his burden in sight of land not far from Athens, he asked the Monkey if he were an Athenian. The latter replied that he was, and that he was descended from one of the noblest families in that city. The Dolphin then inquired if he knew the Piraeus (the famous harbor of Athens). Supposing that a man was meant, the Monkey answered that he knew him very well and that he was

1. "Aesop's Fables," sec. "Fictions That Point to the Truth," paras. 1–2.

2. Story originally provided by Kathy Beck, Colorado Springs librarian. The best reference for the Aesop's fables is Robert Dodsley's *Select Fables of Esop and Other Fabulists*. ("Esop" is Dodsley's spelling.) The book was originally published in 1761 and has been reissued in various editions by multiple publishers over the years.

an intimate friend. The Dolphin, indignant at these falsehoods, dipped the Monkey under the water and drowned him.

Moral: Bragging, lying, and pretending has cost many a man his life and estate.[3]

Skipping forward a thousand-plus years to the eighth century C.E. and moving from the waters of the Aegean to the sand and shores of the Middle East, we pick up tales from *The Arabian Nights*, aka *The Thousand and One Arabian Nights*. It is the story of Scheherazade, the ever so clever thousandth(!) virgin bride of King Shahryar. Queen for a night, her beheading scheduled for the next morning (as happened to all others before her), Scheherazade tells the king such an intriguing story that he invites her to come back for an unprecedented second night. She does return for a thousand nights rich in story.

The first story she tells—right for this anthology—is given by Sinbad the Sailor. He relates a tale from his sailing days when he and fellow shipmates disembarked to walk about on a mid-ocean, plant-growing island, planning there to wash their clothes. Sinbad tells us,

> We were just deciding that no one could live there, without fresh water, when suddenly Abdul caught sight of a fountain—a geyser, rather—a great distance from us. Its water gushed higher and higher, seemingly the height of a castle tower, then dropped out of sight.
>
> . . .
>
> "The island is sinking!" someone cried.
>
> "The island is moving!" another shouted.
>
> A deep roaring beneath us was followed by a second eruption of water from the geyser. The jet spouted so high that the spray reached us on the wind and soaked us to the skin in a second.

They were on the back of a whale! To make matters worse, a fire they'd started was scorching the whale's back, causing the angry leviathan to sound, thus drowning all the sailors except Sinbad. He escaped, he says, by holding on to the laundry tub. Days later, he floated to an actual island and was rescued finally by a merchant ship.[4]

3. Besides appearing in the Dodsley book (cited above), this identical fable may be found on the website fablesofaesop.com.

4. McCaughrean, *Arabian Nights*, 12–13.

The second watery fable to tell from *The Arabian Nights* is "The Fisherman and the Bottle." Scheherazade says there once was a fisherman who three times cast his net in an ocean bay. The first cast brought in a dead donkey; the second, mud as well as broken pottery shards; and the third, a copper bottle with a lead stopper. With his knife, the fisherman breaks the seal, an immense cloud of smoke escapes, and a giant genie materializes. This genie is beyond mad because he had been trapped in the bottle for 2,000 years with no one to let him out. So, he is looking for revenge on anyone. The fisherman makes for a convenient target. However, before the genie can kill him, the fisherman tricks the genie by asking him to demonstrate how he manages to go in and out of the bottle. The genie shows him, and, when the giant is back inside, the fisherman recaps the copper bottle. Now trapped, the genie, from inside the bottle, promises to help the angler. He directs the man to an inland pond. Going there, the angler catches four large freshwater fish.[5] (The fish caught might well have been carp, for that species originated in the East and, over time, were transplanted west . . . to become the preferred Christmas dinner fare in Eastern Europe.)

Though *Arabian Nights* was penned in the Middle East and *Aesop's Fables* began in Greece, they eventually became known in Western Europe, where they were repeated, adjusted, and expanded. One example of an adapted fable is that told by Englishman Robert Dodsley, 1703–1764, involving salmonoids, called "The Old Trout, the Young Trout, and the Gudgeon." It goes as follows:

> A Fisherman in the month of May stood angling on the bank of the Thames with an artificial fly. He threw his bait with so much art, that a young trout was rushing towards it, when her mother prevented her. "Never," said she, "my child, be too precipitate, where there is a possibility of danger. Take due time to consider, before you risk an action that may be fatal. How know you whether yon appearance be indeed a fly, or the snare of an enemy. Let someone else make the experiment before you. If it be a fly, he will very probably elude the first attack: and the second may be made, if not with success, at least with safety." She had no sooner spoken, than a gudgeon seized the pretended fly, and became an example to the giddy daughter of the importance of her mother's counsel.[6]

5. "The Fisherman and the Bottle," in McCaughrean, *Arabian Nights*, 29–35. A different version of this tale, called "The Story of the Fisherman and the Demon," is in Husain Haddawy's translation *The Arabian Nights*, 30ff. Haddawy's version is based on a 14th-century Syrian manuscript.

6. "The Old Trout, the Young Trout, and the Gudgeon," in Rundell, *Fables of Aesop*,

The moral: "Don't rush into things. Study them first."

In the next century, the 19th, we encounter *Grimms' Fairy Tales,* aka *Children and Household Tales.* In the Grimms' collection are stories quite familiar to readers and listeners, young and old: "Cinderella," "Hansel and Gretel," "Little Red Cap," "Snow White and the Seven Dwarfs," "Rumpelstiltskin," "Rapunzel," "The Pied Piper," "Puss 'n' Boots," "The Town Musicians of Bremen," and others. Having read (in my case, having heard) 210 stories, I have pulled together a composite profile of them, to wit:

> Once upon a time, a king—nobleman or miller—had three sons (almost always three), the youngest of which is the most handsome, noble, or challenged. The youth are sent on impossible missions, which almost invariably take them into an enchanted forest. In that forest, they meet up with witches, dwarves, giants, sorcerers, or evil queens, as well as talking bears, wolves, foxes, or birds that divert or help them on their way. Sometimes, the adventurers, when pursued, are turned into stone or even into a lake or duck or tree or frog or mountain. Almost always the characters—they can be girls, maidens, or princesses—get lost or must climb mountains or cross rivers. They often come to a mysterious grand palace or a woodcutter's humble cottage. Here, they may find a witch or, perhaps, if we're talking about the young men, three beautiful princesses or maidens whose hands they must win by solving riddles, killing a dragon, or recovering a treasure of gold and jewels. At the end, the youngest protagonist and the most beautiful princess join in marriage. They become king and queen and live happily ever after.[7]

The Grimm brothers' tales involving fishing, fish, and water are several. They follow much of the formula suggested above with anthropomorphism, magic, repetition, and a moral lesson. Consider the tale "The Fisherman and His Wife," which, necessarily, I condense in this retelling:

> A poor fisherman, who lived with his wife in a pigsty, one day caught a flounder that talked. The magic fish, which he released, told the man he could have any wish he wanted. The man, quite content with his life, could think of nothing. When he got home

---

297–98.

7. The composite description was created by the author after listening on BARD to dozens of tales.

and told his wife about the talking fish, she told him to go back and ask for a cottage. He went, singing,

“Flounder, flounder in the sea,
Come, I pray thee, here to me.
For my wife, good Ilsabil,
Wills not as I'd have her will.”
or, this alternative incantation:
“Flounder, flounder in the sea
If you're a man, then speak to me
Though I don't agree with my wife's request,
I've come to ask it, none the less.”

The fish appeared, and the fisherman presented his wife's request. When he got home, the pigsty had become a comfortable cottage. The wife, though, wanted more, so she sent the man back to ask for a brick house. The fisherman repeated the call; the fish heard and granted the wish.

The Fisherman and His Wife

> Well, this goes on for some time while the sea gets rougher and rougher. Still, the wife desires more and gets a mansion with many servants. Next, she asks to be king in a castle with armies at her command and a crown of gold and diamonds. Next, she wills to be emperor and, finally, pope. All is granted. Last of all, she wills that the fish make her as God, able to control the rising and setting of the sun.[8]

Perhaps the "be as God" request was granted, for she found herself with her poor fisherman-husband back in the pigsty[9]—God, after all, "emptied himself" (Philippians 2:7) and was born in a lowly cow shed.

This Brothers Grimm fairy tale has a Russian version called "The Golden Fish." Here the fisherman's incantation is

> Head in air and tail in sea,
> Fish, fish, listen to me.

The Russian version also has the fisherman's wife asking for "more, bigger, and better" things, all leading to a similar humbling conclusion.[10]

In these fables, as in some others, there is a "blame it on the woman" motif, as in the biblical Adam and Eve story. Doubtless, that may be because men wrote the fables. The larger theme of human dissatisfaction and greed is the nongendered and universal lesson.

The Grimm Brothers' tales and the Russian fable happen to lift up the contemporary ethic of catch-and-release. Fishing waters do bless anglers if fishers are not greedy and return some of their catch to their home . . . which may be another moral to be drawn from these stories.

Still, one more fable, this one from Iran, called "The Two Fishermen and the Three Fishes":

> There was once in your Majesty's dominions a certain pond, the water of which was very clear, and emptied itself into a neighboring river. This pond was in a quiet place; it was remote from the highway, and there were in it three Fishes; the one of which was prudent, the second had but a little wit, and the third was a mere fool. One day, by chance, two fishermen, in their walks, perceiving this pond, made up to it, and no sooner observed these three Fishes, which were large and fat, but they went and

8. The fable "The Fisherman and His Wife" may be read in the Harvard Classics volume *Folk-Lore and Fable*, 83–90.

9. One version says that they find themselves "back in a piss pot"!

10. For a quite humorous, 21st-century retelling of this fable, see "The Frog Who Liked to Fish" in Erik Forrest Jackson's *Fairy Tales From the Brothers Grimm*, 197–230. Here, the fisherman is the Muppets' Kermit the Frog, and the wife is Miss Piggy!

fetched their nets to take them. The Fishes suspecting, by what they saw of the Fishermen, that they intended no less than their destruction, began to be in a world of terror. The prudent Fish immediately resolved what course to take; he threw himself out of the pond, through the little channel that opened into the river, and so made his escape. The next morning the two Fishermen returned; they made it their first business to stop up all the passages, to prevent the Fishes from getting out, and were making preparations for taking them. The half-witted Fish now heartily repented that he had not followed his companion: at length, however, he bethought himself of a stratagem; he appeared upon the surface of the water with his belly upward and feigned to be dead. The Fishermen, also having taken him up, thought him really what he counterfeited himself to be, so threw him again into the water. And the last, which was the foolish Fish, seeing himself pressed by the Fishermen, sunk down to the bottom of the pond, shifted up and down from place to place, but could not avoid at last falling into their hands, and was that day made part of a public entertainment.[11]

11. Story in *The Fables of Pilpay*, 99. It is a 19th-century reworking of a tale in *The Arabian Nights.*

Chapter 3

Biblical and Saintly Stories

The third genre of fishy and watery tales in this review of stories focuses on those in the Bible, on those of the Christian saints, and on others from Christian history. Many of these stories are better known than the fables and cultural tales covered in the previous two chapters.

Let's begin with tales from the Bible. Biblical water and sea tales are relatively few because the Jews and Christians of old were not maritime people. They were, in fact, quite wary of the deep, it being the dark and mysterious realm of God. Even so, in Genesis 1:1, we hear about God "brooding over the deep," and, while creating,

> God said, "Let the waters bring forth swarms of living creatures, and let birds fly above the earth across the dome of the sky." So God created the great sea monsters and every living creature that moves, of every kind, with which the waters swarm, and every winged bird of every kind. And God saw that it was good. God blessed them, saying, "Be fruitful and multiply and fill the waters in the seas, and let birds multiply on the earth." And there was evening and there was morning, the fifth day.[1]

In Chapters 6 through 9 of that first book of the Bible, we learn about Noah and the great flood. As the story goes, because of humankind's widespread wickedness, God decides to drown all the people on Earth except for one righteous man and his family. That man is Noah. God warns Noah of the coming deluge, so Noah builds an ark, cubit by cubit, onto which he, his wife, his sons and his sons' wives, as well as creatures, including birds, come on board, male and female, two by two. (Fish—safe in water and perhaps not so wicked—are not mentioned.) The rain arrives and continues for 40 days after which the rain stops, the water recedes, and repopulation begins.

1. Genesis 1:20–23.

This biblical flood story, recorded around 700 B.C.E., may have been inspired by the 2100 B.C.E. Babylonian deluge account suggested in *The Epic of Gilgamesh*, recounted in Chapter 1 of this book.[2]

Although the authors of the Bible were not seafaring people, from time to time, they acknowledge the importance of the sea to transport people as well as wheat, wine, pottery, and other items, as suggested in Psalm 107:23–31, which reads, in part, "Some went out on the sea in ships." Besides going out for commerce, communication, and empire-building, ancient folks, as today, took to the seas to catch fish, always in awe of the big ones.

Sea monsters are mentioned in Genesis 1, and the great sea creature Leviathan is considered in several places in the Bible—Isaiah, Amos, Job, and the apocryphal Book of Enoch. Sometimes, Leviathan is portrayed as a fire-breathing underwater monster and, in other places, as simply a big fish or a whale. In Job 1:1–2, dumbfounding angling questions are asked of Job,

> Can you draw out Leviathan with a fishhook
>   or press down its tongue with a cord?
> Can you put a rope in its nose
>   or pierce its jaw with a hook?

Job's silence indicates that he can do none of those things, for, then, perhaps as ever, the big one always gets away.

The best-known fish story in the Bible, of course, is that of Jonah and the whale, which goes something like this: The prophet Jonah, living in Israel, is instructed by God to go and preach in Nineveh, capital of hated Assyria. Not wanting God's word to be heard there, Jonah flees Israel in a boat. On the sea, a storm arises, threatening all on board. Jonah acknowledges that God has caused it because he was disobeying God. So, the sailors throw Jonah overboard. Immediately, the storm abates, and a giant fish swallows him. The fish swims him to shore, where the reluctant prophet is spit out. Now, Jonah goes to Nineveh, as commanded, where, ironically, they worshiped Dagon, the fish god, as well as the fish goddess Nanshe.[3]

2. Other cultures and times also have tales of a great flood. The Roman poet Ovid (20 B.C.E. to 18 C.E.) in *Metamorphoses* tells of a flood where the fish were swimming up the elm trees! Ovid's flood story echoes an earlier Greek account. Flood stories have been told in Polynesia, China, India, Iran, Africa, America (South and North), seemingly everywhere. Our current century has begun with myriad experiences of devastating floods, many as a result of human-caused climate change.

3. For further information on these Assyrian gods, see "Who Was Dagon in the Bible?"

Jonah Swallowed by a Great Fish

The tale of Jonah and the whale is found in Jonah 1 and 2 and has been widely retold throughout the centuries in fine art, folk art, Sunday-school flannel boards, and literature. *The Adventures of Pinocchio,* for example, include a version of this biblical tale and is recounted in Chapter 8 of this book.

In some Bibles, between the Old and New Testaments, can be found the Apocrypha, which tells the best fish tale in all scripture. The story is in the Book of Tobit.[4] I reconstruct it as follows: Tobit's son, Tobias, is sent by his blind father from Nineveh, where the family lives, on a mission to Media, there to retrieve money belonging to the father. Tobias is accompanied by a dog (the only pet mentioned in the Bible) and by the angel Raphael. At the River Tigris, while wading in the water, a fish attacks the young man's toe. Instructed by Raphael, Tobias catches the fish and throws it on the bank, where they roast it. Raphael tells Tobias to save the fish's heart, liver, and gallbladder for medicine. Upon arriving in Media, the pair encounter relatives of Tobias, including the beautiful Sarah, who has had seven would-be

4. The Book of Tobit is one of the Deuterocanonical books, also known as the Apocrypha. It is generally not included among Protestant Christians' list of canonical texts while Roman Catholics and most Orthodox traditions include it.

husbands murdered on their wedding nights by the demon Asmodeus. Even so, Tobias wants to marry Sarah. A wedding is arranged, and, on their first night, per Raphael's instructions, Tobias burns the earlier-caught fish's heart and liver over red-hot embers. This causes horrible-smelling smoke that repels the demon and drives him off to the Egyptian desert, allowing Tobias and Sarah to consummate their marriage. Meanwhile, Raphael retrieves Tobit's money, and the three—four if you count the dog—return to Nineveh. There, Tobias rubs his father's eyes with the fish's gallbladder, and the old man's cataracts are removed, allowing him to see clearly.

The Bible's New Testament also has some fishing-fish-water accounts. Most of them involve Jesus. Among the first is that of Jesus choosing his disciples. Early one morning, Jesus is walking along the shore of the Sea of Galilee when he sees some men fishing in their boats. He asks how they are doing, and they report that they have been catchless all night. Jesus advises, "Cast your net on the right side of the boat." When they do, they bring in what is usually called "the miraculous draught of fishes." This account appears in Luke 5:4–11. A post-resurrection version of the miraculous-draught tale can be found in John 21:1–14. When Peter and the other fishing disciples come ashore, hauling their net behind them, they find the resurrected Jesus on the shore, offering bread and fish to the crowd. John tells us the number of fish caught that day was 153, a significant number but for what reason there is no consensus.

The story of the miraculous draught is also spun as the parable of the loaves and fishes. In this account, a great crowd had gathered to hear Jesus speak. His disciples wondered how to feed the large numbers, since inquiry had revealed that they had only five barley loaves and two small fish—the provisions belonging to a young boy in the crowd. Jesus blesses the offering, which then feeds more than five thousand.

Another fish story involving Jesus and his disciples is found in Matthew 17:24–27:

> When they reached Capernaum, the collectors of the temple tax came to Peter and said, "Does your teacher not pay the temple tax?" He said, "Yes, he does." And when he came home, Jesus spoke of it first, asking, "What do you think, Simon? From whom do kings of the earth take toll or tribute? From their children or from others?" When Peter said, "From others," Jesus said to him, "Then, the children are free. However, so that we do

> not give offense to them, go to the sea, and cast a hook; take the first fish that comes up, and, when you open its mouth, you will find a coin; take that and give it to them for you and me."

In 1996, while studying in Israel, my wife and I took a boat ride on the Sea of Galilee and, on its shore, enjoyed a lunch of St. Peter's fish (*Sarotherodon galileus*), which proved quite tasty. In that same year, she and I visited St. Peter's Basilica in Rome, the largest cathedral in the world. While we stood there gawking, some guy in the back of our tour group whispered, "Pretty nice tomb for a fisherman!"

The biblical stories cited above involve fish, fishing, people, and one thing more—water. In the Bible as a whole, water is mentioned 722 times. Water figures prominently throughout the New Testament, from Jesus' baptism in the River Jordan to the Book of Revelation's vision of the "river of the water of life . . . flowing from the throne of God" (Revelation 22:1). In between those two references is much else to do about water—for example, Jesus walking on it, people being baptized in it, a cold cup of it offered to a little one, that which came from Jesus' pierced side when he was on the cross, and St. Paul sailing on it.

All of which is to say, in the New Testament, fishers, fishing, fish, and water play prominent roles. The most significant story is in the word "fish" itself. In the early Christian church, centuries before the cross became Christianity's primary symbol, the symbol of choice was the fish. The Greek word for fish, IXTHUS or ICTHUS, became an acronym for the essential Christian story: I/Jesus X/C/Christ [is] THeo's/God's Uius/Son [and] Soter/Savior. That makes for a 2,000-year-old fish tale in which many have played a part, and, for which, this author has been a narrative preacher.

Moving somewhat beyond the Bible's pages, we come upon what could be termed "saint stories." Given that the fish was the first symbol of Christianity, right beside it might be a sailing ship, suggesting the spread of Christianity over the waters of the Earth. At the end of Jesus' life and ministry, he says to his disciples, "Go into all the world and preach the gospel" (Mark 28:19). And they did, especially by means of sailing ships that took them around the Mediterranean Sea. The Book of Acts says that St. Paul went to Greece and, eventually, to Rome as did St. Peter. Getting there, Paul was shipwrecked. Peter's brother, Andrew, also went to Greece, where, tradition has it, he was martyred, becoming that country's patron saint. Later, his bones were taken to Scotland, where he is also a patron saint. Andrew's symbol is an X-shaped cross, sometimes shown as two fish diagonally crossed. Even today, a white X on an ocean-blue background is the pattern of the flag of Scotland.

St. James the Greater, brother of Jesus, died in Jerusalem, but his body, by legend, was transported to Spain in—of all things—a *stone* boat! He is Spain's patron saint. St. John and Jesus' mother, Mary, traveled to Ephesus in present-day Turkey, where they are honored. Sailing from the Mediterranean into the Aegean Sea through the Dardanelles Strait into the Black Sea and around to Armenia was St. Bartholomew, aka Nathaniel.[5] Armenia became the first country to adopt Christianity as its religion. St. Mark, as the story goes, went to Egypt and became its patron saint. Mary Magdalene became such in France. Most of the Christian saints reached their destinations by ship.

Though anything about St. Simon the Zealot and his travels is obscure, his symbol is a fish on a Bible. St. Jude's symbol is a boat; he is reputed to have traveled widely, Odessa on the Black Sea being one of his docking ports. Thomas the Apostle is said to have traveled the Persian Gulf to plant Christianity in India, especially among the fisher caste. Later, followers of Christ from Syria crossed the Red Sea to establish Ethiopian Christianity.

Whether Jesus' disciples—or others after them—ever actively wet a line or cast a net on their travels is not recorded. In their wide seafaring, however, they likely did fish by one means or another, as seafood was a staple in the diet of the ancients.

In the fifth century C.E., a Christian youth named Patrick, living in Roman Britain, was captured by pirates and transported to Ireland, where he was made a slave and forced to care for goats. After six years, he managed to escape by boat back to England—and, then, France, where he became a priest. Eventually, he returned to Ireland by boat, introducing Christ as the legendary Salmon of Knowledge, whose tale has been told in Chapter 1 of this book. The lad became St. Patrick, widely honored on the traditional day of his death—March 17.

From Ireland in the sixth century C.E., there arose the account of Brendan the Navigator, one of the Twelve Apostles of Ireland and the most popular Irish saint after Patrick. As the story goes, Brendan and 14 fellow monks set off in a boat of leather stretched over a wooden frame. They sailed, singing to God,

> Thy way is the sea,
> and thy path is the great waters,

5. There is trout fishing in contemporary Armenia, as noted in the book *The Towers of Trebizond*, reviewed in Chapter 11 of this anthology. Perhaps there also was some in St. Bartholomew's time, second century C.E.

> and thy footsteps are not known.[6]

They went west in search of the Isle of Blessing, that is, Paradise. On their wind-guided journey, they came to sundry islands, those of birds, of grapes, of bread-providers, of a solitary monk, of mountains spewing fire (Iceland?), of smiths, and of sheep. The isle of sheep had "large streams of water, full of fish, flowing from various springs,"[7] likely salmon, available to be caught and eaten fresh or salted for later consumption. Brendan and his crew had many exciting adventures, some mishaps, and many pious moments. Here is a fish-rich passage from John O'Meara's *The Voyage of St. Brendan*:

> It happened on one occasion that as Brendan was celebrating the feast of Saint Peter the Apostle in his boat, they found the sea so clear that they could see whatever was underneath them. When they looked into the deep they saw the different kinds of fish lying on the sand below. It also seemed to them that they could touch them with their hands, so clear was that sea. They were so numerous that they looked like a city of circles as they lay, their heads touching their tails. . . .
>
> [Brendan] began to intone as loudly as he could. Others of the brothers kept their eyes on the fish all the time. When the fish heard him singing, they came up from the bottom and began to swim in a circle round the boat—in such a way that the brothers could not see beyond the fish anywhere, so great was the multitude of the different fishes swimming. Still they did not come near the boat, but kept swimming at a distance in a wide arc. And so they kept swimming here and there until the man of God had finished Mass. After this, as if they were taking flight, they all swam by different paths of the ocean.[8]

At one treeless island, they stopped for dinner. When the island began to move, they realized something was wrong. The sailing party scrambled back to the relative safety of their coracle. Brendan then told the brothers,

> "My sons do not be afraid. God revealed to me during the night in a vision the secret of this affair. Where we were was not an island but a fish—the fore-most of all that swim in the ocean. He is always trying to bring his tail to meet his head, but he cannot because of his length. His name is Jasconius.[9]

6. Psalm 77:19.
7. O'Meara, *Voyage of St. Brendan*, 33.
8. O'Meara, *Voyage of St. Brendan*, 68–70.
9. O'Meara, *Voyage of St. Brendan*, 36.

At one point, in *The Voyage of St. Brendan*, the monks are pursued by a monster who, in turn, is cut into three pieces by an even more powerful, fire-breathing fish.[10] The brothers later ate that fish.

In some versions of Brendan's journey, the sailors traveled to the New World, possibly Newfoundland, and, from there, made their way south to Florida! (This is all legend, of course—Irish, to be sure.) After six years, Brendan's group returned to the Emerald Isle to tell and retell their whale-riding and other adventures. Understandably, Brendan became the patron saint of whales and whalers.

Another holy man of Ireland was St. Kevin of Glendalough (498–618!). After being ordained to the priesthood, Kevin spent seven years as a hermit in the mountains surrounding Glendalough, living in a small cave. His life was spent in prayer and self-denial, and he lived off herbs and fish. In winter, Kevin visited the lake, where he would stand up to his neck in the ice-cold water to pray. During one of these sessions of prayer, he dropped his breviary into the lake. An otter appeared from the bottom of the lake with the prayer book, unstained or damaged in any way, in its mouth. Henceforth, the otter would bring fish to Kevin for food and later brought fish to feed Kevin's fellow monks.[11]

Another fishy saint story is that of St. Corentin of Brittany. This one is also from the sixth century C.E. St. Corentin's hermitage was in the woods beside a little pool. In the pool lived a little fish. The fish admired the monk's devotion. So, one day, when Corentin was coming off a 40-day fast, the fish offered himself for the saint's table. St. Corentin accepted the generous offer. When the meal was finished, the monk threw the fish's bones into the pool. Here, the bones regenerated into another fish for another day's meal. The routine was repeated, and the monk never lacked for a meal although perhaps he wished for more variety in his repasts.

One day, King Gralon, the pagan ruler of Brittany, came by Corentin's hut with 50 soldiers. He asked for all to be fed. Corentin gave them his daily fish, and the single fish multiplied in their mouths. King Gralon was so impressed by the miracle—and by the monk's preaching—that he converted to Christianity and established a bishopric in the nearby town of Quimper, where Corentin became the first prelate. Most assuredly, St. Corentin's feeding of the 50 soldiers is a twist on the Bible story of Jesus feeding 5,000.

10. O'Meara, *Voyage of St. Brendan,* 56–59.

11. "Kevin of Glendalough."

A far-fetched saintly tale to pair with that of St. Corentin is that of St. Anthony of Padua.[12] This one comes from the 13th century C.E. and is found in the book *The Little Flowers of Saint Francis*. As the story goes, Anthony traveled in northern Italy to preach, but his words won no converts. So, he turned from the land to the sea, in particular, to where the Marecchia River flows into the Adriatic Sea at the port of Rimini. Here, he began his sermon. Little fish with their heads out of the water lined up to listen. Middle-sized fish fell in behind, and, behind them, large fish lined up in the deep water. The miracle pulled the people in, even the heretics, and "all came to believe in the true Catholic faith." When it was all over, St. Anthony "blessed the fish before they swam away. And as they left, they were expressing their joy with gladness in the sea."[13]

St. Francis of Assisi, after whom *The Little Flowers* is named, made a seafaring trip in 1219. He sailed from Italy to Egypt in an attempt both to convert Sultan Al-Kamil and to put an end to the Fifth Crusade. He did not succeed on either front, so Francis sailed home. Back in Italy, he befriended, and was befriended by, birds and other wildlife. Francis blessed them, but the records do not say if those blessed animals included sea creatures. I only know that, one year in my congregation, on the feast day of St. Francis (October 4), when we blessed children's pets, one girl brought forward a goldfish in a jar!

Beginning in the late 15th century, Portuguese and Spanish navigators sought new lands for their countries and sovereigns. Navigators from other nations—the Netherlands, France, and England—soon followed. These explorers usually were accompanied by clergy. Shipboard and on newly discovered lands, the religious observed holy communion. Whether by Catholic transubstantiation or in a simple Quaker memorial meal, Jesus—FISH/IXTHUS—was lifted up in sacred ritual.

In time, Europeans came to live, work, and worship in the new worlds. One such group came to North America—the Pilgrims. Their experiences provide us with two fish stories to end this chapter. The first one is short but significant: From the land's indigenous people, the Pilgrims learned to fertilize crops with dried fish, which add nitrogen and other nutrients to the soil. The second story is related to the first Thanksgiving in 1621. In

12. This St. Anthony, please note, is of Padua, not Anthony "of the desert" (fourth century C.E., Egypt).

13. *Complete Francis of Assisi*, 350.

recounting this event, William Bradford, the governor of Plymouth Colony, remembered that they had venison (provided by indigenous hunters), turkey, and fish—in particular, bass and cod. On other days, Eastern brook trout and other species likely were caught for table fare.

It is by boat, of course, that the Pilgrims got to America, and it is largely by boat that Christianity initially spread around the world to eventually "net" over two billion adherents. Understandably, then, the symbol of the World Council of Churches is a boat afloat on the sea with its mast in the form of a cross.

The biblical and saintly stories considered above, extended by those of later faithful folk, are from Jewish and Christian sources. Doubtless, similar fishy tales exist in other faith traditions—Buddhism, Islam, Hinduism, etc. Collection of them could be wonderfully rewarding, but such would have taken this author farther afield—or, a-water—than this book is wont to go.

Chapter 4

Classic Literature

Classic literature—although likely not primarily about fish, fishing or water—may provide a tale or passage within their larger narratives that rightly fit within this book's collection.

The Epic of Gilgamesh, considered in Chapter 1 of this book, is the starting point for recorded literature in the West.[1] As noted, prior to Gilgamesh's unearthing in 1853, Homer's *The Iliad* and *The Odyssey* were thought to be the West's oldest writing. A millennium after Homer, the Latin poet Virgil (70–19 B.C.E.) retells *The Odyssey* in *The Aeneid.* Therein, the Trojan hero-warrior Aeneas, like Odysseus, has many perilous encounters, finally arriving home in Italy, preparing the way for the founding of Rome. Nothing of fishing or fish is mentioned in Virgil's epic—only water quite dangerous.

The classic Roman poet who may have written about fishing is Ovid (43 B.C.E.–18 C.E.). Attributed to him is the fragmentary poem *Halieutica* (*On Fishing*), but the authorial hand may have belonged to a later writer, and what exists is not particularly fishy. In his poem *The Art of Love,* however, Ovid notes that wooing a lover and catching a fish both involve the same thing—deception.

Other ancient Roman writers focused more clearly on fishing, including fly fishing, than what is contained in *Halieutica* or *The Art of Love.* For such, we will need to look to the writings of Martial and Aelian, coming up in Chapter 7.

1. An Egyptian funerary text, *Book of the Dead,* written on papyrus, is older than *The Epic of Gilgamesh,* but the funerary text consists of prayers, not stories. Extant copies of *Book of the Dead* date from around 1500 B.C.E., and some of its material likely came from the third millennium B.C.E.

Leaving behind the ancient Greek and Roman writers, we move toward the Middle Ages. The sixth-century historian Procopius of Caesarea reported a monster fish—perhaps an errant sperm whale—plowing the Black Sea for 50 years, wreaking havoc. This is according to Herman Melville in *Moby Dick*.[2] Certainly, there was inland freshwater and ocean fishing in those times, but scant literature exists to tell us about it. A notable exception to this paucity has been picked up by fishing historian Mark Kurlansky:

> The oldest-known writing on fishing in England, The Colloquy of Aelfric, dates from 995. In this book, a tenth-century abbot named Aelfric, archbishop of Canterbury, known for his writing in Anglo-Saxon, makes clear that fishing is about commerce, not sport. The fisherman in his colloquy states that the purpose of fishing is "food, clothing, and money." He expresses his preference for river fishing over fishing at sea and says of whaling, "I would rather catch a fish I can kill than one that can kill me." He also expresses a distaste for rowing.[3]

As for the best-known medieval authors, neither the Venerable Bede, who wrote *Ecclesiastical History of the English People* (731 C.E.), nor the oldest piece of French literature, *The Song of Roland* from the 11th century, nor Geoffrey Chaucer, who gave us *The Canterbury Tales* (1392), talk about fishing or anything particularly watery. Still, we know ships plied the European waterways, carrying grain, goods, and people. Celtic monks traveled the Atlantic in the sixth century as did the Vikings, 793–1066. As for fishing-related literature from these medieval folk, as noted, there is little. However, various aquatic species certainly were fished for, notably cod from the Atlantic Ocean by seafaring Basques. Knowing well how to preserve their catches with salt, they became known as the fish merchants of Europe.[4] Would that the Basques had given us written tales of their harvesting!

There is, however, a true story from the 13th century C.E. that suggests fish and fishing. At that time, the head of the Roman Catholic Church received and started wearing a signet ring. That ring is known as the Ring of the Fisherman or the Piscatory Ring and features a bas-relief of St. Peter in a boat, hauling in fish with a net. Since at least Pope Clement IV, every pope has received such a band. The Fisherman Ring of the former pope is defaced at the end of a pontificate, and a new ring created.

Let us now widen our net, so to speak, to find fish stories from other parts of the globe.

2. Melville, *Moby Dick* (1989), 193–94.
3. Kurlansky, *Unreasonable Virtue of Fly Fishing* (2019), 157.
4. Kurlansky, *Cod*, "Part One: A Fish Tale," 19ff. on the Basque fishermen.

As a child, I knew that fishing was not simply an American pastime or occupation. Eating from Blue Willow dishware, I imagined that the little Asian fisherman on my plate had a story worth knowing. After all, the man, standing on a bridge, held a pole with a little fish dangling on the line.

The fish heads carved on Inuit totem poles certainly were inspired by stories. Polynesians and Amazonians have great fishing stories as well. These tales, transmitted by oral tradition, only later were recorded and made available to readers. Chapter 1 of this book has some of these legendary tales, which would be considered "classic" in their culture.

The breakthrough book that opened up fly fishing to readers appeared in 1496. It was Dame Juliana Berners' *A Treatyse of Fysshynge Wyth an Angle*. As it is especially informative and instructive in character, not classic like others we have under consideration here, I treat her book more fully in Chapter 7.

The truly classic book on fly fishing for all time comes 150 years after Dame Juliana's *Treatyse*. It is Izaak Walton's *The Compleat Angler*. Aside from the Bible, *The Compleat Angler* is, if you can believe it, the most-read book in the English language, besting any single offering of William Shakespeare or Jane Austen.

With *The Compleat Angler*, we get a fishing book not unlike those that many modern angling authors pen. The storyline of the book has the author, called Piscator, going "a-fishing" within walking distance of London on English chalk streams, such as Severn, Trent, and Essex, tributaries of the Thames. His traveling companion is Venator, a hunter of game. A fowler, called Auceps, joins the two. Each sportsman speaks of the worth of his avocation, angling finally given primary consideration. Eventually, Piscator and Venator go it alone. Below are two fishing tales within the book. The first describes the taking of a chub.

> Pisc. Look you here, sir, do you see? (but you must stand very close), there lie upon the top of the water, in this very hole, twenty chubs. I'll catch only one, and that shall be the biggest of them all; and that I will do so, I'll hold you twenty to one, and you shall see it done.
>
> Ven. Ay, marry, sir, now you talk like an artist, and I'll say you are one, when I shall see you perform what you say you can do; but I yet doubt it.
>
> Pisc. You shall not doubt it long, for you shall see me do it presently: look, the biggest of these chubs has had some bruise

> upon his tail by a pike, or some other accident, and that looks like a white spot; that very chub I mean to put into your hands presently; sit you but down in the shade, and stay but a little while, and I'll warrant you I'll bring him to you.
>
> Ven. I'll sit down, and hope well, because you seem to be so confident.
>
> Pisc. Look you, sir, there is a trial of my skill, there he is, that very chub that I showed you with the white spot on his tail: and I'll be as certain to make him a good dish of meat as I was to catch him. I'll now lead you to an honest ale-house where we shall find a cleanly room, lavender in the windows, and twenty ballads stuck about the wall; there my hostess (which, I may tell you, is both cleanly and handsome, and civil) hath dressed many a one for me, and shall now dress it after my fashion, and I warrant it good meat.[5]

The second story involves a trout, likely a German brown.

> Pisc. And now you shall see me try my skill to catch a trout; and at my next walking, either this evening or tomorrow morning, I will give you direction how you yourself shall fish for him.
>
> Ven. Trust me, master, I see now it is a harder matter to catch a trout than a chub: for I have put on patience, and followed you these two hours, and not seen a fish stir, neither at your minnow nor your worm.
>
> Pisc. Well, scholar, you must endure worse luck some time, or you will never make a good angler. But what say you now? There is a trout now, and a good one too, if I can but hold him, and two or three more turns will tire him. Now you see he lies still, and the sleight is to land him. Reach me that landing net; so, sir, now he is mine own, what say you now? Is not this worth all my labour and your patience?
>
> Ven. On my word, master, this is a gallant trout.[6]

Coming in from fishing across a meadow, Piscator and Venator meet the milkmaid Maudlin and her mother. In exchange for a fresh-caught chub, Maudlin sings them a song that begins, "Come live with me and be my love."[7] The song is one of many poems in the book, the most fishing-related being "The Angler's Song," containing a bit of story in itself:

5. Walton, *Compleat Angler*, 66.
6. Walton, *Compleat Angler*, 80.
7. Marlowe, "Passionate Shepherd to His Love."

O the gallant fisher's life,
It is the best of any!
'Tis full of pleasure, void of strife,
And 'tis beloved by many:
Other joys
Are but toys;
Only this
Lawful is;
For our skill
Breeds no ill,
But content and pleasure.

In a morning up we rise
Ere Aurora's peeping;
Drink a cup to wash our eyes;
Leave the sluggard sleeping,
Then we go
To and fro
With our knacks
At our backs
To such streams
As the Thames,
If we have the leisure.

When we please to walk abroad
For our recreation,
In the fields is our abode,
Full of delectation:
Where in a brook,
With a hook,
Or a lake,
Fish we take;
There we sit
For a bit,
Till we fish entangle.[8]

Having hooked (pun intended) Venator, actually the Englishman Charles Cotton, on the merits of angling, Piscator, who is the author Izaak Walton, then takes 21 chapters to educate his student about fishing—describing fish of the river, baits needed, and instruction on how to catch, dress, and cook various species. Hereby, the reader, too, learns about chavender or chub, umber or grayling, salmon, pike, carp, bream, tench, peach,

8. Walton, *Compleat Angler*, 183–84. I listened to "The Angler's Song" on BARD that seems to have even more water references than does the print version.

barbel, gudgeon, bleak, roach, dace, and others. Piscator recommends a variety of flies, offering instructions on how to tie them and what months to use them.[9] All are "wet" flies that are used below the water's surface. Ground baits, such as worms, grubs, and grasshoppers, also are recommended, not to forget minnows called pinks.

All along, Walton references ancients, authors, divines, scientists, and friends who angle or have observations of the natural world: Pliny, St. Augustine, Conrad Gessner, Francis Bacon, and lesser knowns. Parts of the Bible are regularly quoted, and attribution to God is given for life and beauty. Walton often says grace. The reader also gets acquainted with English rural life, including inns, food, and drink. I especially love these lines from *The Compleat Angler* that have Piscator saying to Venator, whom he calls Scholar:

> Indeed, my good scholar, we may say of angling, as Dr. Boteler said of strawberries, "Doubtless God could have made a better berry, but doubtless God never did"; and so (if I might be judge) "God never did make a more calm, quiet, innocent recreation than angling."[10]

Part 2 of *The Compleat Angler* is like Part 1, but the authorial hand is that of Charles Cotton, formerly referred to as Venator. Cotton now becomes Viator and travels on horseback with a new guide, Piscator Junior, who claims Sir Izaak as his father. The two men travel by horseback into County Derbyshire (northwest England) and cross the River Why[11] en route to the River Dove, where they fish. Piscator Junior recommends flies for each month, calling special attention to the green drake and the stonefly for June and July. They meet no milkmaids, but Cotton's fishing hut, called "the temple," is their residence one night. (That same hut still stands beside the River Dove.)

The book closes with a scripture, I Thessalonians 4:11, "Study to be quiet." Perhaps this means "strive to live a quiet life" for which angling may be helpful.

9. Dame Juliana Berners, who is fully introduced in Chapter 7, may have set the pattern for Walton and Cotton regarding recommendations on flies to tie and use, month by month.

10. Walton, *Compleat Angler*, 114.

11. From which, no doubt, David James Duncan drew the title of his 1983 novel, *The River Why*.

A hint of Walton's *The Compleat Angler* appears in one of England's greatest novels, *Middlemarch* by George Eliot (the pseudonym of Mary Ann Evans), published in full in 1872. Eliot's story focuses on English provincial life around 1830, and it touches on fly fishing. Sir James Chettam, a rejected suitor, is attempting to persuade his rector, Humphrey Cadwallader, to intervene in the engagement of the girl whom Chettam loves. That girl, Dorothea, is about to marry the Reverend Edward Casaubon, a man much older than she. Rector Cadwallader's wife, having overheard the two men's conversation, notes,

> "But you will make no impression on Humphrey. As long as the fish rise to his bait, everybody is what he ought to be. Bless you, Casaubon has got a trout stream, and does not care about fishing in it himself: could there be a better fellow?"
>
> "Well, there is something in that," said the Rector [Cadwallader], with his quiet inward laugh. "It is a very good quality in a man to have a trout stream."[12]

The Reverend Cadwallader, who fiddles with fishing tackle, likely angled on a chalk stream with flies, just as Izaak Walton, 200 years earlier, recommended that a proper Englishman do.

Let us now shift away from British authors and attend to three 19th-century American novelists who have generated classic literature that is related to fishing and water: Herman Melville, Henry David Thoreau, and Mark Twain.

With little disagreement, the most powerful fishing tale ever told and one of America's greatest novels is Herman Melville's *Moby-Dick; or, The Whale*. First published in 1851, it begins with the well-known words "Call me Ishmael." The book is Ishmael's narrative of the obsessive quest of Ahab, captain of the whaling ship *Pequod*, for revenge on Moby Dick, a giant white sperm whale that bit off his leg at the knee. Thereafter, Ahab hobbled bitterly on a peg leg made of whale bone. The book acquaints the reader with fish and whaling, ships and boats, nautical riggings, oceans of the world, and the improbable men who sailed on them. Melville draws heavily on the Bible and Shakespeare for language and images. Here is a beautiful and ominous passage:

> Consider the subtleness of the sea; how its most dreaded creatures glide under water, unapparent for the most part, and

12. Eliot, *Middlemarch*, 70.

> treacherously hidden beneath the loveliest tints of azure. Consider also the devilish brilliance and beauty of many of its most remorseless tribes, as the dainty embellished shape of many species of sharks. Consider, once more, the universal cannibalism of the sea; all whose creature's prey upon each other, carrying on eternal war since the world began.
>
> Consider all this; and then turn to the green, gentle, and most docile earth; consider them both, the sea and the land; and do you not find a strange analogy to something in yourself? For as this appalling ocean surrounds the verdant land, so in the soul of man there lies one insular Tahiti, full of peace and joy, but encompassed by all the horrors of the half-known life. God keep thee! Push not off from that isle, thou canst never return![13]

There was one, Melville tells his readers, who pushed off from that safe, green isle—Captain Ahab in search of his nemesis, Moby Dick. One of the most intriguing questions in this long and complex novel is who or what the white whale represents. Is Moby the personification of evil, as Ahab thinks, or is he a benign creature with no malicious intent? Or could he be, somehow, "God, provoked"? One online commentator says, "To Ahab, we might conclude, the White Whale represents the power that limits and controls man. Or, maybe he is just a big, smart fish."[14]

In *Moby Dick*, the most exciting and calamitous fishing account appears at the end of the novel. Chapter 133,"The Chase—First Day," reports that the white whale is finally located after two years and an all-oceans search. At the time of spotting the whale, the sea is peaceful and serene, and the whale's white hump stands out like something in a Greek myth. The whaling boats are lowered from the *Pequod* to chase after Moby. In charge of each boat is one of the ship's officers: Starbuck, Stubb, Flask, Ahab. Harpooners Queequeg (a tattooed Pacific Islander), Tashtego (a Native American from Gay Head), and Daggoo (a tall West African) are each in a boat's bow. In Ahab's boat is the sinister Parsee named Fedallah.

When Moby is reached, the beast lifts himself out of the water in an arc and dives into the deep. The boatmen wait for him to return from the sounding. The whale suddenly surfaces and, jaws open, presses hard toward Ahab's boat. Ahab quickly steers his boat away from the whale and takes his harpoon in hand. Moby, however, rolls aside and, from beneath, takes the boat in his jaws, shaking it as a cat would shake a mouse. Melville writes,

13. Melville, *Moby Dick* (1989), 246–47. The pages that now follow, presented with few actual quotations, are drawn from this Reader's Digest version of the book, especially pages 464–89, "The Chase" chapters.

14. "Critical Essays Major Symbols in *Moby-Dick*," para. 9.

"Both jaws, like enormous shears, bit the craft completely in twain." One of the whale's enormous teeth is right next to Ahab's head, and the men can't stab at the whale with their harpoons because its body is under the boat. Ahab struggles with the whale but is thrown into the open sea, his whalebone leg shattered. Still, no one drowns that first day.

On day two, the harpooners, including Ahab and Fedallah in a new boat, succeed in placing lances in the whale. The barbs madden the animal, and he overturns all the boats, wildly scrambling harpoon lines. Fedallah, Ahab's personal harpooner, gets entangled in ropes and is pulled behind the whale, where his corpse trails for more than a day. All the others, however, manage to survive. The ship's carpenter cobbles together yet another boat for Ahab, in which Ishmael, the story's narrator, will ride.

On day three of the hunt, Moby Dick is harpooned by Ahab. In a fury, the whale then attacks the *Pequod* itself, smashing it apart, causing it to sink. In his smaller boat, Ahab is encircled by Moby and entangled with the harpoon rope. It goes around his neck as a hangman's noose. He is pulled off the boat and down to the depths. All others on board the *Pequod* and Ahab's whaleboat drown in the maelstrom. Only Ishmael, floating on a wooden casket constructed for his shipmate Queequeg, survives to tell the tragic story.[15]

Pegleg Captain Ahab Carried Off by Moby Dick

15. The story behind *Moby Dick*, specifically the destruction of the *Pequod* by a whale,

"'Tis quite a tale," theologians, English professors, and thoughtful readers—including fishers—will agree. However, at the time of its publication in 1851, *Moby Dick* went largely unnoticed, and its author, Melville, would die essentially unrecognized. Likewise, Melville's contemporary, Henry David Thoreau, died never knowing he had penned what also was a masterwork. We now turn to it.

After many years of writing and rewriting, Henry Thoreau's *Walden; or, Life in the Woods* was published in 1854. It sold barely 300 copies and went unheralded until after Thoreau's death in 1864 and, really, until the 20th century. Today, though, *Walden* is widely read and critically acclaimed. Countless readers resonate with these famous words:

> I went to the woods because I wished to live deliberately, to front only the essential facts of life, and see if I could not learn what it had to teach, and not, when I came to die, discover that I had not lived.[16]

Part of Thoreau's way of living simply and deliberately involved angling. He tells us that, occasionally, after his hoeing was done for the day, he went "a-fishing." Sometimes, he went with an elderly neighbor who also enjoyed the pond. On warm evenings, Thoreau drifted about in his boat, playing the flute and observing the perch circling below him. Thus, he spent many days and nights, enjoying idyllic contentment and ease.

At the beginning of his chapter "The Ponds," Thoreau informs us that, while fishing at night, he felt that a powerful integration of the human and the transcendent was occurring within himself:

> It was very queer, especially in dark nights, when your thoughts had wandered to vast and cosmogonic themes in other spheres, to feel this faint jerk [on the line], which came to interrupt your dreams and link you to Nature again. It seemed as if I might next cast my line upward into the air, as well as downward into this element which was scarcely more dense. Thus I caught two fishes, as it were, with one hook.[17]

Transcendentalist Thoreau's fishing line connects his two worlds, the worlds of Nature and of Spirit.

In the chapter "The Pond in Winter," Thoreau gives us the following description of fishing and fish:

---

is based on the actual 1820 sinking of the whaleship *Essex*. Nathaniel Philbrick's book *In the Heart of the Sea: The Tragedy of the Whaleship Essex* recounts that disaster.

16. Thoreau, *Walden and Civil Disobedience*, 72.

17. Thoreau, *Walden and Civil Disobedience*, 146.

> Early in the morning, while all things are crisp with frost, men come with fishing-reels and slender lunch, and let down their fine lines through the snowy field to take pickerel and perch; wild men. . . . They sit and eat their luncheon in stout fear-naughts on the dry oak leaves on the shore. Here is one fishing for pickerel with grown perch for bait. You look into his pail with wonder as into a summer pond, as if he kept summer locked up at home, or knew where she had retreated. How, pray, did he get these in midwinter? Oh, he got worms out of rotten logs. . . . The perch swallows the grub-worm, the pickerel swallows the perch, and the fisher-man swallows the pickerel; and so all the chinks in the scale of being are filled.
>
> When I strolled around the pond in misty weather, I was sometimes amused by the primitive mode which some ruder fisherman had adopted. He would perhaps have placed alder branches over the narrow holes in the ice, which were four or five rods apart and an equal distance from the shore, and having fastened the end of the line to a stick to prevent its being pulled through, have passed the slack line over a twig of the alder, a foot or more above the ice, and tied a dry oak leaf to it, which, being pulled down, would show when he had a bite. . . . Ah, the pickerel of Walden! When I see them lying on the ice, or in the well which the fisherman cuts in the ice, making a little hole to admit the water, I am always surprised by their rare beauty, as if they were fabulous fishes. . . . They are not green like the pines, nor gray like the stones, nor blue like the sky; but they have, to my eyes, if possible, yet rarer colors, like flowers and precious stones, as if they were the pearls, the animalized nuclei or crystals of the Walden water. They, of course, are Walden all over and all through; are themselves small Waldens in the animal kingdom, Waldenses. It is surprising that they are caught here—that in this deep and capacious spring, far beneath the rattling teams and chaises and tinkling sleighs that travel the Walden road, this great gold and emerald fish swims.[18]

What a deep appreciation of fish and fishing Thoreau expresses in his classic memoir!

While living on Walden Pond (1846–47), Thoreau made a trip to Maine with the hope of climbing Mount Katahdin, the highest peak in the state at nearly 5,300 feet. He tells about his trip in the book *The Maine Woods.* Guided by "Uncle George" McCauslin, Henry and his party made their way up the Penobscot River with many portages. Nearing their destination, the

18. "The Pond in Winter," in Thoreau, *Walden.*

party went fishing. Here are passages about angling the confluence of the Murch Brook and Aboljacknagesic mountain streams:

> We had been told by McCauslin that we should here find trout enough; so, while some prepared the camp, the rest fell to fishing. Seizing the birch poles which some party of Indians, or white hunters, had left on the shore, and baiting our hooks with pork, and with trout, as soon as they were caught, we cast our lines into the mouth of the Aboljacknagesic . . . . Instantly a shoal of white chivin (Leuciscus pulchellus), silvery roaches, cousin-trout, or what not, large and small, prowling thereabouts, fell upon our bait, and one after another were landed amidst the bushes. Anon their cousins, the true trout, took their turn, and alternately the speckled trout, and the silvery roaches, swallowed the bait as fast as we could throw in; and the finest specimens of both that I have ever seen, the largest one weighing three pounds, were heaved upon the shore . . . .[19]

Thoreau also reports on his fishing the next morning:

> In the night I dreamed of trout-fishing; and, when at length I awoke, it seemed a fable . . . I doubted if I had not dreamed it all. So I arose before dawn to test its truth, while my companions were still sleeping. There stood Ktaadn with distinct and cloudless outline in the moonlight; and the rippling of the rapids was the only sound to break the stillness. Standing on the shore, I once more cast my line into the stream, and found the dream to be real and the fable true. The speckled trout[20] and silvery roach, like flying-fish, sped swiftly through the moonlight air, describing bright arcs on the dark side of Ktaadn, until moonlight, now fading into daylight, brought satiety to my mind, and the minds of my companions, who had joined me.[21]

Thoreau ends with this fishing wrap-up:

> By six o'clock, having mounted our packs and a good blanketful of trout, ready dressed, and swung up such baggage and provision as we wished to leave behind upon the tops of saplings, to

19. Thoreau, *Maine Woods*, 47–48.

20. Thoreau's trout were, to be sure, brook trout, since German browns from England and rainbows from the Pacific Northwest were not introduced into New England waters until the late 1800s.

21. Thoreau, *Maine Woods*, 49–50.

> be out of the reach of bears, we started for the summit of the mountain . . . .[22]

No doubt, on the way up, the trout were skewered over hot coals and enjoyed for lunch.

Along with Melville and Thoreau stands another 19th-century literary giant—Mark Twain. His tales do not involve the ocean or mountain streams but a mighty river, the Mississippi. Neither do his tales involve whale or trout, but, rather, species found in mid-American warm waters—bass, perch, and catfish. This piscine episode is extracted from Twain's enduringly popular novel *The Adventures of Tom Sawyer,* published in 1876:

> While [Injun] Joe was slicing bacon for breakfast, Tom and Huck asked him to hold on a minute; they stepped to a promising nook in the river-bank and threw in their lines; almost immediately they had reward. Joe had not had time to get impatient before they were back again with some handsome bass, a couple of sun-perch and a small catfish—provisions enough for quite a family. They fried the fish with the bacon, and were astonished; for no fish had ever seemed so delicious before. They did not know that the quicker a fresh-water fish is on the fire after he is caught the better he is . . . .[23]

Such is the truth that anglers, enjoying fried fish at a shore meal, readily will attest while adding tales of their own to Twain's.

Still considering classic literature, let us shift away from American authors and go back to Europe for seafaring novels considered classic. From the early 18th century and continuing well into the 19th, we have adventure tales that involve water and could involve angling. Consider Daniel Defoe's 1719 *Robinson Crusoe.* To survive, surely Crusoe would have fished, but, in Defoe's telling, the survivor never did, just shot or tamed wild goats for food.

Another relevant novel is *Gulliver's Travels* or *Travels Into Several Remote Nations of the World.* Written by Jonathan Swift, an Anglo-Irish cleric, and first published in 1726, it is a satirical parody on European—especially British—culture, ethics, pretensions, and politics. Swift's storyteller is Lemuel Gulliver, a ship's doctor. On Gulliver's first voyage, his ship is blown off course to wreck on an unchartered island called Lilliput. There, he is, first of

22. Thoreau, *Maine Woods,* 50.

23. Twain, *Adventures of Tom Sawyer,* ch. 14, p. 96.

all, bound by its inhabitants, who stand only six inches high. Later, Gulliver hears the Lilliputian parliament debate the important matter of which end of an egg to crack when making an omelet. On his second voyage, he lands on Brobdingnag, an island of moral giants, 60 feet tall, who refuse Gulliver's offer to teach them about gunpowder. On his third adventure, Japanese pirates cast him off to an island that floats in the air and is inhabited by scientists, mathematicians, and musicians, who, despite their talents, are not particularly admirable. Gulliver's last significant stop is a land governed by talkative, intelligent horses called Houyhnhnms, who are inarguably superior to the humanlike creatures of the island called Yahoos. The water for Gulliver's voyages is likely the South Pacific if anyplace.[24]

Fish are incidentally mentioned in Robert Louis Stevenson's 1883 *Treasure Island*. Fishing accounts are present in Johann David Wyss' 1812 *Swiss Family Robinson*, to wit:

> Ernest had not been absent long, when I heard him cry out, "Papa! papa! a huge fish! I cannot hold it; it will break my line." I ran to his assistance, and found him lying on the ground on his face, tugging at his line, to which an enormous salmon was attached, that had nearly pulled him into the water. I let it have a little more line, then drew it gently into a shallow, and secured it. It appeared about fifteen pounds weight; and we pleased ourselves with the idea of presenting this to our good cook.[25]

Jules Verne's 1869 book, *20,000 Leagues Under the Sea*, has an exciting man-and-fish episode and, later, a man-and-giant-squid encounter. In *20,000 Leagues*, a French naturalist, Professor Pierre Aronnax, along with Conseil, his assistant and a classifier of biological species, and harpooner Ned Land board a frigate on a several-ocean search for an occasionally spotted giant narwhal. When finally encountered, the whale turns out to be a submarine. The sub sinks the frigate. The three men, however, are picked up from the wreckage and taken on board the *Nautilus*. The submarine's skipper, Captain Nemo, is a strange—though not necessarily malevolent—explorer. He has sworn never to return to land. So it is that Nemo transports the virtual captives on an eight-month voyage of 69,767 miles or 20,000 leagues. They navigate mostly underneath the surface, sometimes down several miles, traveling at speeds up to 43 knots or almost 50 miles per hour. (This is science fiction after all.) The submarine goes many places: to the lost continent of Atlantis, to open water at the South Pole, through an unknown

24. Swift, *Gulliver's Travels*. My retelling is based upon listening to the book on BARD.

25. Wyss, *Swiss Family Robinson*.

tunnel running from the Red Sea to the Mediterranean, and through other watery passages. Looking through glass panels and examining dragnet findings, Aronnax and Conseil see and classify hundreds of fish, plants, corals, shells, crustaceans, and geologic formations—most of the classifications accurate, at least by 19th-century knowledge. The only species Jules Verne seemed to have missed are euryhalines—fish adaptable to water of various salinities, such as salmon and steelhead trout.

One exciting fish encounter takes place during an exploration of the pearl-oyster beds off Ceylon, now Sri Lanka. Using diving suits with compressed-air tanks, no less, Nemo, Aronnax, Conseil, and Ned Land explore the oyster beds. While doing so, they spot an Indian fisherman, diving for oysters from a skiff. Holding a heavy stone with his feet, the diver descends to the bottom on a rope. Once there, he quickly loosens oysters, stuffs them in a sack, drops the stone, and then ascends the rope. Hidden behind a ledge, the four explorers from the *Nautilus* observe him, Aronnax reporting,

> I kept watching him very closely. He worked with speed and precision. For half an hour, no danger seemed to threaten him. I was somewhat taken by the spectacle of that interesting manner of pearl fishing when suddenly, while the Indian was on his knees, I saw him make a gesture of terror, get up quickly, ready to spring to the surface.
>
> I understood that terror! A gigantic shadow appeared above that unfortunate diver. It was a shark of huge dimensions, moving speedily toward him with his jaws wide open and fire in his eyes!
>
> I was mute with horror, completely paralyzed. With a vigorous blow of his fin, the voracious monster shot toward the Indian, who jumped to one side and avoided the shark's bite. But he could not avoid the monster's tail, which struck him on the chest and threw him flat on the ocean floor. This scene had scarcely lasted more than a few seconds. Then the animal, turning over, came back, ready to cut the poor man in two, when I saw Captain Nemo, who was next to me, suddenly get up and, dagger in hand, make straight for the monster, ready to fight it hand-to-hand.
>
> Just as the shark was ready to snap the unhappy diver in two, he saw his new adversary, and turning over, made straight for him.
>
> I can still see the posture of Captain Nemo. Bracing himself, and with admirable sangfroid, he waited for the formidable enemy, and when the monster lunged at him, he sidestepped with incredible speed, avoided the jaws of the animal, and plunged

> his dagger into the belly of the monster. The battle was not over, however. A terrible struggle followed.
>
> The shark seemed to roar, as it were. Blood poured from its wounds. The water turned red, and through those darkened waters I no longer saw anything.
>
> Nothing, until the clear spot appeared in the water, when I saw the intrepid Captain holding fast to one of the fins, still struggling hand-in-hand with the monster, riddling, with blows of his dagger, the belly of the enemy, but unable to reach his heart. The shark churned the water so furiously that the rocking almost upset me. I would've liked to help the Captain, but paralyzed with horror, I was unable to move.
>
> I looked on with dread. I saw the battle take a new turn. The Captain fell on the ground, brought down by the enormous weight of the creature. The shark's jaws opened wide, like a shearing machine, and it would have been all over with the Captain if Ned Land, with the speed of lightning, had not rushed forward and struck it with his harpoon. The waves were a mass of blood. The shark beat them with an indescribable fury. Ned Land, however, had not missed. This was the monster's death battle. Struck to the heart, it struggled with frightful convulsions, whose shocks knocked Conseil down.[26]

Another dramatic man-versus-sea-creature encounter, told at the end of the book, occurs when a giant squid attacks the *Nautilus*, endangering all on board and carrying off one of the ship's men. This monster-of-the-deep encounter inspired dramatic art for movie-house posters.

One exceedingly popular 1897 novel—certainly "classic" for boys—is *Captains Courageous*, written by British author Rudyard Kipling and extolled by Teddy Roosevelt. The story—involving fishing, fish, and water—features a rich, spoiled 15-year-old boy, Harvey Cheyne Jr., en route to Europe on a steamship with his mother. Harvey falls overboard, and, when the disappearance is discovered, it is presumed the young man drowned. The crew of the fishing schooner *We're Here*, however, working the Grand Banks of Newfoundland, rescues him. Harvey asks the fishing smack's captain, Disko Troop, to return him to port in Gloucester, saying his millionaire father certainly would reward the captain handsomely. Not believing the lad's story,

26. Verne, *20,000 Leagues Under the Sea*. I listened to the book on BARD; this excerpt is found in part 2, ch. 3.

Captain Troop tells the boy that he must fish alongside the crew for the entire three-month season. Harvey is promised a seaman's salary ($10.50 a month) and is put to tasks on the boat. He works with the old salts—learning ropes, rigging, and onboard protocols. The captain's same-age son and Harvey become fast friends, working and fishing together. Here is an account of one day's angling out of the *We're Here* dory:

> Harvey smiled at the thought of his ten and a half dollars a month and wondered what his mother would say if she could see him hanging over the edge of a fishing-dory in mid-ocean . . . . Suddenly the line flashed through his hand, stinging even through the "nippers," the woolen cadets supposed to protect it.
>
> "He's a logy. Give him room accordin' to his strength," cried Dan. "I'll help ye."
>
> "No, you won't," Harvey snapped, as he hung on to the line. "It's my first fish. Is it a whale?"
>
> "Halibut, mebbe."
>
> Dan peered down into the water alongside, and flourished the big "muckle," ready for all chances. Something white and oval flickered and fluttered through the green. "I'll lay my wage an' share he's over a hundred. Are you so everlastin' anxious to land him alone?"
>
> Harvey's knuckles were raw and bleeding where they had been hanged against the gunwale; his face was purple-blue between excitement and exertion; he dripped with sweat, and was half-blinded from staring at the circling sunlit ripples about the swiftly moving line. The boys were tired long ere the halibut, who took charge of them and the dory for the next twenty minutes. But the big flat fish was gaffed and hauled in at last.
>
> "Beginner's luck," said Dan, wiping his forehead. "He's all of a hundred."
>
> Harvey looked at the huge gray-and-mottled creature with unspeakable pride.[27]

On the schooner, Harvey and the crew encounter whales, brave storms, and witness a fishing skiff cut apart by an ocean liner. By the story's end, Harvey has become a strong and capable lad, made so by fellowship, hard work, and good luck on the high seas.

Although other authors may have given us excellent fishing-fish-water stories worthy of inclusion within this genre, those presented above are adequately illustrative.

27. Kipling, *Captains Courageous*, 38.

Chapter 5

Existential and Spiritual Offerings

Fishing, fish, and water stories can be found in a fifth genre of literature—novels, novellas, memoirs, and movies that are contemporary, deeply human, and, what I would call, "existential." They could be—and often are—fictional, but that doesn't mean that they aren't truth-filled, believable, or relevant. These stories are often social-psychological, philosophical, even theological. Family dynamics are frequently a critical story component. Some offerings in this genre are

James Dodson, *Faithful Travelers*

David James Duncan, *The River Why*

Jeannette Haien, *The All of It*

Ernest Hemingway, "Big Two-Hearted River" and *The Old Man and the Sea*

Norman Maclean, *A River Runs Through It*

Harry Middleton, *The Earth Is Enough: Growing Up in a World of Flyfishing, Trout, and Old Men*

Tim O'Brien, *The Things They Carried*

Howell Raines, *Fly Fishing Through the Midlife Crisis*

The stories and books above stand out as exemplary existential literature dealing with fish, but, certainly, there are many other offerings that also treat weighty matters of this life. For example, *The Epic of Gilgamesh*, the opening tale in this collection, concerns a man's desperate quest for immortality.

Whereas Melville's *Moby Dick* concerned questions of good and evil as well as God, Ernest Hemingway's 1925 story "Big Two-Hearted River" takes up Hamlet's provocative question—whether "to be or not to be?" In "Big Two-Hearted River," the protagonist, Nick Adams, an emotionally damaged World War I veteran, goes deep into the burnt-over woods of Michigan to find himself—or, perhaps, to lose himself. He camps beside a river that Hemingway repeatedly refers to as "black." Here, he catches grasshoppers and goes fishing, misses a big trout but finally captures two keepers. At one point, smoking a cigarette and eating an onion sandwich, Nick contemplates going into the deep water of the swamp. Instead, "at the log in the river, he guts and cleans the two trout before returning to camp."[1] Without an explicit explanation, the reader realizes that something more than a mere walk in the woods has happened. Was shell-shocked Nick considering suicide? If so, a couple of good trout caught and cleaned seem to pull him back.

Downhearted Nick Adams on the Big Two-Hearted River

1. "Big Two-Hearted River," in Lyons, *Hemingway on Fishing*, 23–24.

Hemingway's novella *The Old Man and the Sea* is another nonpareil story. This tale of one man's persistence, courage, and acceptance begins as follows:

> He was an old man who fished alone in a skiff in the Gulf Stream, and he had gone eighty-four days now without taking a fish. In the first forty days a boy had been with him. But after forty days without a fish the boy's parents had told him [not to go with the old man again].[2]

On his 85th day, old Santiago ventured much farther out to sea. There, his bait is taken by a giant marlin that Santiago comes to call his brother. Then, for two full days, the fish pulls him away from land, only submitting on the third day. During a lull in the long fight, Santiago manages to catch a small fish that he eats raw. On the arduous return to Havana, sharks attack the marlin tied to the side of the skiff. Despite the old man's valiant efforts to ward off the sharks, they devour the flesh of his fish. Santiago returns home with only skeletal evidence of his once-great trophy. The bones of the monster are left on the shore, where, the next day, bypassing tourists take the remains to be that of a shark, totally unaware of the history of those 16 feet of bones. However, Santiago's young fishing companion and his parents may understand, for, the next day, the lad is allowed to go to sea again with the old man.

The Old Man and the Sea is a powerful tale of human courage for which Hemingway won both a Pulitzer and a Nobel prize.

Now let us consider what I believe is the best fly-fishing story ever told, Norman Maclean's semi-autobiographical *A River Runs Through It*. Maclean's novella begins delightfully with these words:

> In our family, there was no clear line between religion and fly-fishing. We lived at the junction of great trout rivers in western Montana, and our father was a Presbyterian minister and a fly fisherman who tied his own flies and taught others. He told us about Christ's disciples being fishermen, and we were left to assume, as my brother and I did, that all first-class fishermen on the Sea of Galilee were fly fishermen and that John, the favorite, was a dry-fly fisherman.[3]

2. Hemingway, *Old Man and the Sea*, 9.
3. Maclean, *River Runs Through It*, 1.

There are marvelous shorter stories within Maclean's larger narrative. One that I particularly enjoy occurs when brothers Paul and Norman take Norman's vain brother-in-law, a worm fisherman, on a day trip. In addition to his worm can, the brother-in-law brings along Old Rawhide, the town whore. She and he drink up all of the group's beer, get drunk and naked, and fall asleep face down in the sun, getting burned head to heels. When Norman and Paul come upon the naked pair, they discover that Old Rawhide has "LO" tattooed on one buttock and "VE" on the other!

Another time, the brothers Maclean and their father share a fishing day on the Big Blackfoot River. Here, they all take fine fish, Paul catching the largest. As Norman and the Reverend Maclean watch Paul "shadow cast"—that is, cast artistically in a way that doesn't let his line touch the water—the father says of Paul, "He is beautiful."[4] At the end of the day, Paul received some of his dad's rare praise and responded with "I'm pretty good with a rod, but I need three more years before I can think like a fish."[5]

He doesn't get those years, however, for Paul, in addition to being an extraordinary fisherman, is a compulsive high-stakes gambler who is deeply and dangerously behind in paying his gaming debts. One morning, Paul, the beautiful fisher, is found dead in a Helena, Montana, alley—murdered.

Try as he might—and he tried—Norman could not save his brother. About this, he writes,

> In the loneliness of the canyon I knew there were others like me who had brothers they did not understand but wanted to help. We are probably those referred to as "our brother's keepers," possessed of one of the oldest and possibly one of the most futile and certainly one of the most haunting instincts. It will not let us go."[6]

In a sermon, years later, the Reverend Maclean reflects,

> Each one of us here today will at one time in our lives look upon a loved one who is in need and ask the same question: We are willing to help, Lord, but what, if anything, is needed? For it is true we can seldom help those closest to us. Either we don't know what part of ourselves to give or, more often than not, the part we have to give is not wanted. And so it is those we live with and should know elude us. But we can still love them—we can love completely without complete understanding.[7]

4. Maclean, *River Runs Through It*, 155.
5. Maclean, *River Runs Through It*, 157.
6. These words are drawn from the Robert Redford film of *A River Runs Through It*.
7. Redford, *River Runs Through It*.

In Maclean's soulful words, I find a special resonance, for I recognize them to be true of my relationship with my younger brother who has spent too many years in a federal prison.

Of all the angling literature that I have ever read, the powerful words ending Maclean's *A River Runs Through It* have hit me at the deepest level, oft bringing tears despite my familiarity with them. I have recited them in every sermon that I have offered at the funerals for angler friends.

> Of course, now I am too old to be much of a fisherman, and now of course I usually fish the big waters alone, although some friends think I shouldn't. Like many fly fishermen in western Montana, where the summer days are almost Arctic in length, I often do not start fishing until the cool of the evening. Then, in the Arctic half-light of the canyon, all existence fades to a being with my soul and memories and the sounds of the Big Blackfoot River and a four-count rhythm and the hope that a fish will rise.
>
> Eventually, all things merge into one, and a river runs through it. The river was cut by the world's great flood and runs over rocks from the basement of time. On some of the rocks are timeless raindrops. Under the rocks are the words, and some of the words are theirs.
>
> I am haunted by waters.[8]

I tend to interpret the book's closing line, "I am haunted by waters," as "I am made whole by waters" because that has always been true for me, and I know that I am not alone in my response to nature, especially its water.

Right alongside Maclean's novella in excellence is David James Duncan's novel *The River Why*. It's about love, nature, river fishing, openness to God, and a young man's search to find himself. The story tells of Gus Orviston, a recent high-school graduate who lives in Portland, Oregon, with his parents and younger brother, Bill Bob. His fishing father is Henning Hale-Orviston, "H2O," a tweedy, dry-fly, catch-and-release purist. Gus' mother, Ma, is a no-nonsense, dedicated catch-keep-and-eat bait fisher. The parents are ever arguing about the right way to fish, each of their ways allowed in *The Compleat Angler*. Disgusted with the disputes, Gus flees the home and takes up residence in a cabin alongside an Oregon river, the River Why, whose meanderings seem to spell its name. Gus establishes what seems a perfect life of eating, sleeping, and fishing. To support himself, he ties flies, makes

8. Maclean, *River Runs Through It*, 161.

rods, and sells them. However, his idyllic daily routine is broken when he finds the body of a drowned fisherman. Gus, with great difficulty, swims the body to shore. Afterward, he begins to question the meaning of life and how best to live it. In time, Gus meets a philosophically inclined man named Titus and his dog, Descartes. He also meets a young family who model living together peaceably. As significant, Gus develops a fly-tying, rod-building relationship with a much older fisherman named Nick. Nick acquaints Gus with the Norwegian fisherman's prayer, which begins thus:

> The first fish I take
> In the name of Christ,
> King of the Elements,
> The poor man shall have for his need;
> And the King of Fishers,
> He will afterward give me His blessing,
> and still for me the crests of the waves. . . .[9]

As the two work together, Gus observes that his friend has a deep scar in the palm of his hand and that he wears a large fish hook on a cord beneath his shirt, but neither speak of the scar or the pendant until the evening of Nick's departure to set up a fly shop for himself in British Columbia. Then, Gus asks him about the scar and the fish hook. Here is my first-person retelling of Nick's story:

> During World War II, I was serving on a minesweeper in the North Atlantic. At that time, I, as a nonbeliever, would argue with our ship's chaplain, who preached about "the Fisher of Men who calmed the sea." I cursed such talk and told the chaplain, "Take your piety and Bible and go swim it down your Death-god's throat!" Not long after my cursing, a terrible storm arose off the coast of Norway, and our boat struck a drifting mine, blew up, and sank, killing most of those on board. Along with a few others, I was knocked into the frigid, giant waves of the ocean. We all would have drowned had not a Norwegian fishing trawler been in the area. The trawler's crew had two life preservers on short ropes, which they threw to struggling men, pulling them in, but they couldn't reach me. As the trawler plowed away, however, a fisherman on board took a stout fishing rod and cast a line, float, weight, and heavy hook right over my head. I grabbed it, and, as the line ran through my near-frozen fingers, the fisherman pointed into the palm of his own hand. I

9. Duncan, *River Why*, 224.

> understood and pressed the hook against my palm. The fisherman set the hook and reeled me in.

After telling the story, Nick exposes the palm of his hand and whispers, "Behold, son. Behold the sign of the Fisher's love for a wooden-headed ass!"[10]

Somewhat like the Gus Orviston "coming to terms with life" story is Harry Middleton's *The Earth Is Enough*. In this memoir with beautifully descriptive prose, the reader meets young Harry, camping with childhood friends on the island of Okinawa, where Harry's father is stationed. On this camping trip, one of Harry's companions finds a World War II Japanese grenade, picks it up, and is blown to pieces. Harry is deeply affected by witnessing that horrendous event, and, in an attempt to relieve his trauma, his parents send him back to the United States. In rural Arkansas, Harry lives with two elderly men—his maternal grandfather, Emerson, and Emerson's brother, Albert—as well as their old dog, Cody. These brothers carry on simply, finding "the earth is enough" for meaningful existence. Subsistence farming, deep and wide reading by lantern light, and good trout fishing suffice for them. With hand-tied dry flies, they fish on Starlight Creek, a tributary that runs through their bucolic thousand-acre property called Trail's End, usually releasing the trout that they catch. In time, young Harry gets a fly rod and becomes a trout fisher himself. One of the stories within the larger narrative involves a third old guy, Elias Wonder, a Native American who was gassed in World War I and lives up the creek from Harry's relatives. Often, Elias fishes with Harry. One day, Elias Wonder tells his young angling companion about "naming" in Indian culture:

> "When I was a boy," he said, "it was the custom among my people that the young men take a wild creature as their cipher, a mark of their approaching manhood, a badge of character. On a raw spring day the young men assembled by the big river that snakes across the prairie. The sun was just rising, and the dawn spread across the vast plains, a land that seemed to reach beyond time itself. And we young men then chose. Fox. Panther. Eagle. Deer. Bear. Horse. When my turn arrived, I said loudly, clearly, proudly, 'Trout.' My father smiled and was not ashamed. From that moment on, the trout and I have been inseparable."[11]

10. Duncan, *River Why*, 230. My summary is drawn from pages 227 to 231.
11. Middleton, *Earth Is Enough*, 240.

Over the course of the book, there are many deaths: Cody the dog dies, then Elias Wonder, shortly followed by Uncle Albert. Finally, when Harry is in college, Grandpa Emerson also passes away. The young man struggles with each of the deaths, but, thanks to time spent trout fishing with his elders and learning the value of life on this good earth, Harry comes to internal peace. After the funeral of Grandpa Emerson, who was the last of the old men, Harry moves to Montana—for trout fishing.

Another story of a young man's movement through life is Tim O'Brien's *The Things They Carried* in which a critical moment of decision is presented. Fishing the Boundary Waters between the United States and Canada, the author weighs his options: to escape into Canada, thus avoiding a war he doesn't believe in, or to return home to be drafted. Finally and with great difficulty, he agonizingly chooses Vietnam. Among the things he carries to war is the memory of the day of fishing when his critical, deeply existential decision was made.

Yet another excellent story with significant ethical issues and one in which salmon angling plays a part is Jeannette Haien's *The All of It*.

The story begins on a rainy morning. Father Declan de Loughry, a long-serving Catholic priest, stands fishing in a salmon stream, pondering the deathbed confession of one of his parishioners. As he was dying, Kevin had confessed that he and his partner, Enda, had been "living a lie" for some 48 years. They were never married, and, as they well knew, living together as an unmarried couple was considered a sin, according to church law, but there is more. During deep conversation in preparation for Kevin's funeral, Enda confesses "the all of it"—that she and Kevin are actually brother and sister![12]

Dark-eyed and still attractive, Enda tells the priest that, from childhood, theirs had been a life of running from their abusive father, hiding their sibling relationship, suffering shame, and working hard to make the best they could of life. Wherever they went, townsfolk assumed they were married, and the pair never corrected the assumption. A rules-following priest should not provide a Christian burial for either of them. However, after listening to Enda's telling of the couple's struggles and her own loneliness—which appears not unlike the loneliness of Father Declan himself—the priest provides the requiem mass for Kevin and, essentially, absolution

12. At this point, the reader may recall the marriage of Zeus to his sister Hera. Similarly, the Egyptian gods Isis and Osiris, brother and sister, were married.

for Enda. Understandably, all this sharing creates a deep bond between the priest and his female parishioner. He is much drawn to Enda—and she to him—but they never allow themselves to touch. Given their shared shame and guilt, is there still a way that something like love can develop?

At the end of this story, Father Declan returns to his river where, all season long, he has had no catches. This last day of the season, he is given an unpromising beat and an inept young ghillie as his fishing companion. As usual, the priest casts and recasts, trying different fly patterns[13] without a take. In the very last minutes of the fishing season in an unpromising cove, using a #12 Connemara Black—a trout fly!—Father Declan catches a salmon weighing a record 24 pounds 10 ounces. It is quite a fight. As twilight falls, he brings the offering to Enda's door. And this is where the story ends—tenderly and with new possibilities for two aging people.[14]

To finish this reporting on existential literature, consider Howell Raines' *Fly Fishing Through the Mid-life Crisis* and James Dodson's *Faithful Travelers.* Both Raines and Dodson are outstanding writers who went through painful divorces and used fly fishing with a young son or daughter to make the world right again. Dodson's "journey of the heart" with his daughter eventually leads them to fish the rivers of Yellowstone, where quiet peace is found.

Not as familiar as the offerings above but still of deep personal significance are these fishing books touching on matters spiritual:

Sven Berlin, *Jonah's Dream: A Meditation on Fishing*

Eric Eiskramer and Michael Atlas, *Fly Fishing—The Sacred Art: Casting the Fly As a Spiritual Practice*

Jody Martin, *The Spirituality of Fly-fishing: An Introduction*

Anthony Surage, *Bringing Back Eden: Meditations of a Fly Fisher*

James W. White, *Fly-fishing the Arctic Circle to Tasmania: A Preacher's Adventures and Reflections*

The titles above suggest that there can be occasions in angling that transcend the physical and become spiritual, even mystical. At such times, "awe" becomes the operative word. The soul is deeply touched. The suggestion

13. In the novella, the reader learns the charming names of many salmon flies: Hairy Mary, Blue Charm, Black Fairy, Snake Tail, Silver Rat, Silver Wilkinson, Abby, Warden's Worry, Thunder-and-Lightning, and Silver Doctor.

14. Haien, *All of It.* My retelling is based upon listening to the book on BARD.

of such deeper meaning is seen in the opening chapter, "The Face of the Waters," of Sven Berlin's book:

> Jonah is my name. I am a solitary person not given to seeking much human company in this life. If anyone appears by the lake or on the bank of a river wherein I may be fishing, like the heron I am in retreat. There are a few friends with whom I would angle—not chosen because I am considered rare company but chosen because they too seem to understand that fishing is a kind of meditation . . . for like any adventure on the brink of the unknown wherein a dream may be caught, the true fisherman is on a search for wisdom—and of that nothing can be spoken. What he does not catch—therein hides the meaning of his long vigil and the purpose of his understanding.[15]

With this thought, a story of fly fishing and spirituality is begun. In the book, Berlin tells the poignant story of his companion and he axing through a last layer of ice:

> Somehow this was a tremendous relief: we had broken the spell: excitement began to well up inside us.
>
> Yet what depths of the soul does
> Jonah's deep-sea line sound!
>
> These words, sounding back like a distant bell tolling in the ocean of Melville's mind, seemed to bless the filament of nylon I let down into the hole cut in the ice, until I felt the vertical spinner touch bottom. . . . I then began to work the wooden pimp slowly. Lift—drop! Lift—drop! As the line ran through the water, a thin film of ice began to form, movement took up fragments and in no time it was as a string of diamonds shot through by the sun. . . . [With the reel frozen solid] the wind-in can be better done by hand. With each lift and pause I felt the expectation of an unknown life tugging gently at the threads that connected our two worlds. This is the moment for which all fishermen long because at last, for that fraction in time, they are being taken, which is the only moment that enables them also to take. Most moments of experience are only possible when there is a resolution of opposites in this way—be it a sign from God, woman or fish.[16]

15. Berlin, *Jonah's Dream*, 1.

16. Berlin, *Jonah's Dream*, 72–73.

My own fishing book has an essay called "Suspects in the Lineup for the Meaning of Fishing." Below are passages from it:

> Some years ago I received a picture postcard that was most provocative. It shows men fishing beneath a twilight sky and the words, "Many men go fishing all of their lives without knowing that it is not fish they are after," attribution Henry David Thoreau. Most fly-fishers, I suspect, have heard the quote.
>
> . . .
>
> The postcard with the quote made me stammer, "Not after fish? How can that be? If it is not fish, then for what have I given so much of my life, spent so many dollars, and in the last 25 years traveled over 100,000 miles? What was I after or should have been after?"
>
> No facile answer can be given, but a goodly number of suspects may be lined up as to what may be beyond the goal of catching fish.[17]

Having said this, I list the "suspects," such as food for the table, escape from workaday life, a sense of accomplishment, quietude, companionship, or, perhaps:

> [E]lation, even excitement, perhaps joy. It is simply the best to hook into a big fish, have him catapult into the air, throwing water as he turns, then scream out to blue water, taking you way into your reel's backing, and dive to the depths, there to shake his head. What a thrill! The adrenaline rush could be what it's all about. To push fishing into deeper socio-psychological consideration, much less philosophical-theological speculation could be beside the point.[18]

But I do push further, closing the essay with this account:

> Some years ago, I visited the Whitney Museum of Western Art in Cody, Wyoming. There I was stopped in my museum wandering by a large oil painting called "The Fisherman." The canvas showed a bare-chested Native American man sitting in the middle of a canoe, his head and body bent forward, looking into the deep. In the fingers of his right hand was a horsehair line going straight down. Where the line broke the surface was an ever-so-slight circle-ripple, the only feel of movement in the painting. There was no hint of breeze on the water, nor stir of leaf in the birch trees. The canoe, the man, the sky—everything—was

17. White, *Fly-fishing the Arctic Circle*, 263–64.

18. White, *Fly-fishing the Arctic Circle*, 266.

> completely calm. Because of that thin cord, however, the viewer still felt there was something moving, something out of sight, beneath the surface, something of great consequence to this fisherman. The fisherman was plumbing the depth.[19]

I hold that fishing, on occasion, "plumbs the depth" and can lead to a mystical connection—life-affirming and life-changing, existentially meaningful.

The human-divine connection through angling is seldom expressed—at least in print—as James David Duncan observes in *The River Why*:

> Who hasn't heard—particularly from fly fishermen, who flaunt their literacy more than their bait-fishing counterparts—references to anglers as the most meditative of sportsmen? We feather-daubers love to echo Izaak Walton's characterization of our pastime as "the contemplative man's recreation," yet in none of the thousands of pages of modern fishing prose I'd ingested had I encountered even the most rudimentary philosophical speculations.[20]

Happily, there are some of those speculations, however rudimentary, in the several works cited just above.

One book that offers these deeper speculations is Wallace J. Nichols' *Blue Mind*. It is an offering both psychological and philosophical about water. The subtitle of *Blue Mind* provides a story in itself: *The Surprising Science That Shows How Being Near, In, On or Under Water Can Make You Happier, More Contented, and Better at What You Do.*

An adequate conclusion of this chapter must point out that many of the novels, novellas, memoirs, and short stories considered above have made it onto the silver screen, e.g., *The Old Man and the Sea, A River Runs Through It,* and *The River Why. The Perfect Storm,* the story of the ill-fated crew of the Andrea Gail, became a film depicting the historic battle between fishermen and the sea.

Producer and director Robert Redford's movie version of *A River Runs Through It* became a box-office hit, pleasing more than just fishers. Along with artfully depicted scenes of casting to, hooking up with, and fighting

19. White, *Fly-fishing the Arctic Circle*, 274.

20. Duncan, *River Why*, 109.

trout, the film does not neglect the book's tragic family dynamics that made it so powerful, soulful, and compelling.

Classic fishing tales considered in Chapter 4 also have made it to movie houses, notably *Moby Dick*, starring Gregory Peck, and *20,000 Leagues Under the Sea*, featuring Kirk Douglas.

Steven Spielberg's 1975 blockbuster movie, *Jaws*, involving a life-taking and life-threatening great white shark, should be noted too.

Another movie in which fish played a part is *On Golden Pond*, based on a play written by Ernest Thompson. In the movie, a fairly angry teenage boy is left by his father's fiancée (played by Jane Fonda) with her retired parents (played by Katharine Hepburn and Henry Fonda). The older couple's summer residence is on a Canadian lake called Golden Pond. Norman, known as "Old Poop" by his wife Ethel, and the lad strike up a guarded relationship that finds them boating and fishing together. In addition to once nearly drowning, the two go after elusive Walter, a giant rainbow trout of the lake. After an extensive tussle, the boy captures the monster, only to let it go. The characters in the movie also let go sufficiently to ease into reconciled relationships.

And, then, there is the 2011 film *Salmon Fishing in the Yemen*, based on the 2007 novel of the same title by Paul Torday. It is a British romantic comedy involving Alfred, a fisheries biologist, and Harriet, a government representative. They work with a wealthy Yemen sheikh to transplant the cold-water fish of Scotland to his desert country. The transplanting almost succeeds. The romance certainly does. And the whole story is almost believable.

The DreamWorks Pictures' logo seen before their films shows a drawing of a young boy fishing for stars from a crescent moon. While watching the cinematic stars, the moviegoer, it is hoped, will take the storyteller's bait for the duration of the film. It's all quite a lovely angling analogy.

One more movie to be mentioned is the 2019 Netflix production *Fisherman's Friends*. It is, like most of the other fish tales already related, about something other than just angling—in this case, a fractured community brought together, sea shanties well-sung, and love. Cornish crab-pot boatmen who sing together are discovered by a London talent scout. After many machinations, the friends find themselves ninth on the United Kingdom's pop-music chart. The group's discoverer, meanwhile, falls in love with one fisherman's daughter and, ultimately, leaves his urban world to be with her beside the sea—matters of the heart are ever existential.

Chapter 6

Outliers

Checking the shelves of a representative bookstore, one will find titles under many classifications, including: Art, Biography, Children's Lit, Health, History, Home, Nature, Politics, Religion, Science, Sci-Fi, Sports, Westerns, Young Adult . . . virtually ad infinitum. In this chapter, I am lifting up four categories that contain fishing, fish, or water stories and that together constitute an "outlier" genre. The four are murder mysteries, romance literature, fantasy tales, and horror stories.

Murder Mysteries

Robert Reid, author of *Casting Into Mystery: Books for a Winter's Night*, says, "Literature is a great river, as long and broad as it is deep. If mystery fiction is a tributary, then fly angling mysteries comprise a cold clear feeder stream."[1] Where, then, to step into that stream?

The search for murder mysteries with fishing-related plots might begin with the most famous mystery novelist of all, Agatha Christie. Her *Murder on the Orient Express* could have an angling-related title, like *Murder on the Fishing Smack Neptune.* But no, nothing like that appears. Likewise, Arthur Conan Doyle could have had Sherlock Holmes solve a *Death on the River Tweed* case. But no. Or how about Lord Peter Wimsey doing investigations in a Dorothy Sayers novel called *Gaudy Back Bay Casting.* Again, no.

Apparently, no major British mystery writer has penned a novel related to fishing, fish, or water. However, American mystery novelists with stories involving fly fishing can be found. Keith McCafferty's *The Royal Wulff Murders* is his first book in a series of six. It is the quintessential example of what might be found within this mystery classification.[2]

1. Reid, "Fly Fishing Mysteries."

2. McCafferty's book is among the first to show up on the Goodreads website when "fly-fishing mystery novels" are sought. Other titles are suggested, but none are

The Royal Wulff Murders story begins with an older fishing guide, Rainbow Sam Meslik, taking a client down Montana's Madison River. The client hooks the body of a dead man. The dead man has a Royal Wulff fishing fly in his lip. Ostensibly, this was an accidental drowning, but the local sheriff, Martha Ettinger, suspects murder, especially after pond—not river—microbes are found in the man's lungs.

Sheriff Martha Ettinger in The Royal Wulff Murders

Another character in the book is an artist, Sean Stranahan, also a fly-fisherman. A barroom singer by the name of Velvet Lafayette, beautiful and sexy, engages Sean to fish the Madison and to inquire whether any anglers

promising. *Sweet Filthy Boy* and *Dirty, Rowdy Things*, both written by Christine Lauren, are, essentially, sex-laced romance novels. *Reel Woman* by Ally Acker sounds like a possibility, but it is about women in early filmmaking.

remember encountering her missing fly-fisher brother. As it turns out, the drowned man was he. But who killed him and why?

Another dimension of the story involves residents living along the riverfront. One of them is a collector of art who commissioned Sean to do some paintings; another is a retired man and his deaf-mute wife; a third is a well-to-do Hollywood producer; and the fourth, a bicyclist who makes knives for a living. The riverfront residents share a hidden pond that adjoins their properties.

As the plot unfolds, Sean and Rainbow Sam go belly-boat fishing, and, while on the lake, Sam is shot but not killed. Thus, the plot thickens with money, fish (healthy and whirling-diseased), family relations, river stocking and control, real-estate manipulation, mountain climbing, and additional murders. At the end, Sean is fishing Quake Lake and what happens is. . . . For the answer, one must seek out the book.[3]

Another novel among the Keith McCafferty's Sean Stranahan mysteries is *The Cold Hearted River*. It begins with the reader being told that, in 1940, a steamer trunk of fishing equipment belonging to Ernest Hemingway was sent from Key West to Ketchum, Idaho. The trunk never arrived, being either lost or stolen in transit. Sixty years later, a woman is found frozen to death in a Montana bear cave—perhaps murdered. In her backpack is a leather fly wallet bearing the initials "EH." Shortly thereafter, a man is found drowned in the Madison River. His hat is Tyrolean, and Tyrol is a region in Germany where Hemingway once fished. A cased, 1933-built, split-bamboo rod, possibly once owned by Hemingway and hidden along the riverbank, is found near the drowned man's body. In the novel, Stranahan travels back to a Michigan fishing lodge where Hemingway's son Jack fished in the 1960s. Once back in Wyoming, we meet a trigger-happy sheriff and an eccentric, memorabilia-collecting, would-be Hemingway-like writer. One of these two might be the murderer. The writer lives in a cabin once occupied by Ernest, author of "Big Two-Hearted River." The cabin is on the Clark's Fork of the Yellowstone River, a river Hemingway called "cold hearted." This novel has some of the same characters who appeared in *The Royal Wulff Murders*: Sheriff Martha Ettinger, tracker Harold Little Feather, fishing guide Sam Meslik, and painter Stranahan.

Royal Wulff and *Cold Hearted* are two excellent fly-fishing murder mysteries, but there are more. Robert Reid, cited at the start of this section, identifies over 30. In addition to the McCafferty books are those of John

3. For a more complete account of this novel and the next, see my write-up "McCafferty Murder Mysteries," accessible through my website, http://www.jameswildenwhite.com.

Galligan, who also has a fly-fishing mystery series. Here is an overview of the plot of his *The Blood Knot*:

> The protagonist, called "The Dog," is now in Livingston, Montana, thinking about fishing the nearby Yellowstone. As usual, he is subsisting on Swisher Sweets, vodka-Tang, and the hope that pretending to forget his past will be enough. He's forged a few tenuous friendships and now finds himself watching from the bank as troubled local girl Jesse Ringer leads D'Ontario Sneed into the swift current of young love. It's sweet really, but some of the locals object to the relationship on the basis of Sneed's skin color. Then, the unthinkable: Wild Jesse is found shot in the head. Sneed is passed out in her car, gun beside him, window seams taped, and engine running. Sneed is hospitalized for severe carbon-monoxide poisoning and can't string together a sentence to defend himself. So, it falls to The Dog to find the real killer.[4]

Reid notes that Keith McCafferty and John Galligan are murder-mystery novelists who "weave elements of fly-fishing into theme and form, plot and character, and weave landscape into the narrative flow."[5]

Reid reviews other fly-fishing murder mysteries. One is *Death on a Cold, Wild River* by Mark C. McGarrity, an Irish-American novelist. In McGarrity's novel, the chief superintendent of the Irish police's elite murder squad investigates the suspicious death of a famous female fly-fishing writer, fishing guide, and fly-shop owner (who happens to be the superintendent's old flame). The action unfolds on Ireland's myth-haunted west coast. The book is, Reid says, "a fly angler's feast with a buffet of salmon fishing and fly tying served with a dram of ancient Celtic mythology."[6]

Another fly-fishing murder mystery that Reid recommends is Peter Heller's *The Painter*. Reid says,

> [It] is an accomplished novel built on a foundation of the mystery genre, featuring Jim Stegner, a man who cannot avoid trouble. It is also a meditation on love and loss, authenticity and celebrity, obsession and inspiration, passion and violence, not to mention the redemptive power of art and fly-fishing. . . . Fly-fishing for wild trout runs through *The Painter* like a Montana spring creek, where much of the action takes place.[7]

4. This quote is an introduction to the book that I heard on BARD.
5. Reid, "Fly Fishing Mysteries."
6. Reid, "Fly Fishing Mysteries."
7. Quotation from the jacket cover of *The Painter*. Actually, there *is* a Jim Stegner

What I, as a fisher and a reader of *The Painter*, found most interesting was that Stegner fished with dry flies at night, which led to mystery-solving clues.

Heller's novel *The River* is also worth reviewing. It tells the story of two Dartmouth College friends who are on a canoe trip through wilderness lakes toward a Canadian river that will take them north to Hudson Bay. Early on, they meet a couple of Texas rednecks going down in an outboard, consuming much booze. They also come upon an exhausted man who tells them his wife was lost upriver. The friends go back to search for her. They find her half-dead, head bashed by a rock. The two friends put the woman in their canoe and start back down the river only to discover that the victim's husband destroyed most of the pair's food provisions and then paddled off. To survive, the friends and the victim live on berries and trout, mostly brookies taken by fly fishing small feeder streams, mostly using Royal Wulffs and pheasant-tail droppers. The threesome also must overcome a giant forest fire and the armed and dangerous husband, who awaits them at a treacherous rapid. Not all make it down to Hudson Bay alive.

Heller also has a more recent book, titled *The Guide*. The titular guide is a fly-fisherman working at an elite private lodge in Colorado. He and a Hollywood female guest uncover a plot of shocking menace.

Award-winning mystery writer C. J. Box, residing in Wyoming, fishing, hunting, and sometimes guiding, occasionally includes fly fishing in his books. None of his, however, qualify as a fly-fishing mystery novel comparable to those of McCafferty or Galligan. I suggest that Box add to his Joe Pickett series *Wind River Unwinding* and make it a thoroughgoing fly-fishing mystery.

Another of many fly-fishing mysteries is *Murder in Cuba* by Dianne Harman. The book jacket promises

> . . . glimpses of Cuba providing a backdrop to this lighthearted murder mystery. Vintage automobiles and other images described by the author resonate with a place frozen in time since Cuba was last open to U.S. tourism. The natural beauty of this island nation also shines through in the story. There's food, too, as in Kelly's Koffee Shop and the other stories in the Cedar Bay Cozy Mystery series. Murder in Cuba also features an introduction to, of all things, fly-fishing. It's an integral part of the story and part of the reason Kelly and her husband, Mike, journey to

---

who lives, paints, and fishes in New Mexico, not Montana. I have seen some of his paintings in Taos.

Cuba. When Dudley Samms, fly-fishing guide, is found murdered, the story is off and running.[8]

To round off this section, note that my clergy colleague Mark Henry Miller has a salmon-fishing mystery called *Murder on Tillamook Bay*.[9] Salmon- and steelhead-fishing guide Tricia Gleason leads fellow investigators to the killer.

Romance Literature

In researching romance fishing stories, two are identified, David James Duncan's *The River Why* and Derek Grzelewski's *The Trout Dreams: A True Romance of Fly-fishing in New Zealand.*

Duncan's novel tells of a love born on the water. Protagonist Gus Orviston, whom we met in the previous chapter, is walking along an Oregon river when he spots a young woman fishing from a branch that hangs over the river. She is wearing cut-off jeans and a halter top that reveals her curves. As Gus watches, a fish takes her bait and pulls out all the line in her hand, her fishing rod being a stripped-down alder sucker with no reel involved. The fish, a steelhead trout, heads upstream. She quickly disrobes, drops the rod in the current, plunges in after it, grabs ahold, and is pulled away. Besides being amazed, Gus is smitten and wants to meet this fisher gal, but she is gone. He advertises for her in the local fishing newspaper and in nearby trout shops. For the longest time, no connection is made. Then, one day, his fisher gal shows up at his door. She tells him that her name is Eddy. They begin fishing together, fall in love, and, eventually, marry. At the wedding, little brother Bill Bob is the best man, and Titus and his dog, Descartes, are the primary witnesses.[10]

As to the Kiwi romance, it is a true story. Grzelewski identifies himself as both a writer and a fly-fishing guide. He reports that a woman named Jennifer travels from Colorado to New Zealand to fly fish with him for a season. He shares his skills and techniques for successful angling with her. Joyfully, they take prize trout. Time together—and falling in love—changes their lives and their fishing forever. Derek and Jennifer embark upon

8. Harman, *Murder in Cuba*, words from the book cover.

9. The book is available from the author at markhmiller@att.net. Miller's other writings include "Reflections on Life, Ministry and Fishing," *Cast Your Nets, Hooked on Life, Road Signs on the Way to Fishing,* and *A River Runs Through Me.*

10. Duncan, *River Why*. See Chapter 5, "Existential and Spiritual Offerings," of this anthology for background on and characters in this story.

angling adventures from the banks of the Clutha River on New Zealand's South Island to the streams of Colorado.

Besides Duncan and Grzelewski, there *ought* to be novelists who have penned romantic stories involving fishers, fish, or water—and not just incidentally. Consider writers whose stories *might* meet this requirement.

Begin with five well-known romance writers: Barbara Cartland, Danielle Steel, Nora Roberts, Rosamunde Pilcher, and Di Morrissey.

Dame Barbara Cartland was a prolific English writer of contemporary and historical romance novels, the latter set primarily during the Victorian and Edwardian periods. Her novels *The Love Pirate*, *Passion in the Sand*, and *Secret Harbour* each suggest watery possibilities. *The Love Pirate* takes the heroine across the Mediterranean and the Red Sea to Malaysian islands. In another Cartland novel, a character is fishing on a Scotland salmon run.

Danielle Steel is an American writer best known for her romance novels. With over 800 million copies of her books sold, she is the bestselling author alive and the fourth-bestselling fiction author of all time. Her novel *Rushing Water* hints of the possibility for review here. However, the "rushing water" in the title refers to the water that comes by hurricane and flood to New York City; there is no trout stream or fishing pole in sight.

Romance novelist Nora Roberts offers the suggestion of fish and water in her Chesapeake Bay Sagas: *Sea Swept*, *Rising Tides*, *Inner Harbor*, and *Chesapeake Blue*. Mostly, though, these books are about family dynamics. *Sea Swept* tells the tale of three brothers—all former juvenile delinquents, all adopted, and all as different as can be. What is watery about this novel is that the family business is boat building, and so, on occasion, the reader sails Chesapeake Bay. If only the opportunity to go after migrating bluefish had presented itself!

Rosamunde Pilcher's novels bring the reader waterward to the coast of Cornwall, the lochs of Scotland, and the Thames near London, there for love triangles and family dynamics to play out. One of Pilcher's novels follows a man who fishes for bonefish on the flats of the Bahamas before returning to England.

Australian Di Morrissey in *The Winter Sea* offers a novel that includes fishing as a profession. Here's a brief synopsis of the book:

> Escaping an unhappy marriage and an unsatisfactory job, Cassie Holloway moves to the little New South Wales coastal town of Whitby Point. Here she meets the Aquino family, whose fishing business was founded by their ancestor, Giuseppe, an Italian immigrant, some ninety years before. Life for Cassie on the southwest coast is sweet as she sets up a successful restaurant and

> falls in love with Giuseppe's great grandson Michael. But when the family patriarch dies, a devastating family secret is revealed which threatens to destroy her dreams. Cassie's future happiness now rests with her quest for the truth.[11]

Morrissey's story, at least, gets the reader within smelling distance of fishermen and fish—smoked, baked, or fried in Cassie's kitchen.

Joseph Monninger has a nonfiction romance story, after a fashion, in *Home Waters: Travels With an Old Friend*. The old friend is a beloved dog; women are incidental to this story. Together, the fisher and his dog wade Blue Ribbon waters of Wyoming and Montana—the Wind and Bighorn rivers especially. In Yellowstone Park, the dog has a serious run-in with a buffalo but escapes. The romance in these pages is not between two humans but between a man and his dog, and, in this story, both rivers and fishing play a major role.

I already have suggested that there ought to be more and better fishy or watery romance stories. Maybe such will come. For some aspiring romance author, I audaciously submit some possible fly-fishing plot lines:

> A coed from Wellesley journeys to Lee's Ferry, Arizona. She's there to complete a senior-year photographic project on the Grand Canyon. She engages a pontoon-boat guide to take her down the Colorado on a five-day float. She, recently jilted and still hurting, is, of course, a beauty, and he, ruggedly handsome, a loner. On their float, she photographs, he fishes, each in his or her own world. Their separateness is broken when she helps him net a large, kip-jawed bow (taken on a weighted #12 Pteronarcys californica stonefly). In that moment of excitement, their eyes meet for the first time and linger longer than expected. On the third day, the two hike up a narrow, seldom-visited canyon. Miles up, they discover Anasazi petroglyphs, including one of a fish! It is, for them, a sign. There, they build a mesquite fire, watch the sun go into a golden set, and exchange their first kiss. That night only one sleeping bag was used. [This romance could be called Anasazi Trout or Anasazi Fire.] In the coming days, the two lovers explore an ancient cliff dwelling and later capsize in a Class IV rapid. At the end of the river journey, the two meet up with a Navajo elder who gives them a sacred blessing: May happiness be your companion and your days together be good and long upon the earth—and on the water.

11. These words are taken from the promotional review of the book that I read on the Internet.

Here are two other romantic plots for the taking:

> After the death of her father, an Alaska fishing-boat captain, beautiful Melissa Goodrich takes over his operation. Crabbing on the high seas, she rescues sailors from a storm-disabled Russian trawler. In doing so, Melissa meets the handsome Captain Alyosha. In port on Kodiak Island, they eat fish 'n' chips, drink vodka and Sarah Pale-ale, fish for coho salmon, and fall in love. Their love, however, must weather CIA and KGB suspicions and harassment. It does survive, however, and, at story's end, the two are at home in neutral Tahiti.

and

> Cheril Castle is a beautiful divorcee, guiding fishers on the Snake River out of Jackson, Wyoming. She is pursued by both a hunk from Nebraska (who is a worm fisherman) and by a rich dry-fly purist from Vermont (who is an alcoholic). She takes each beau fly fishing in her McKenzie River drift boat but, finally, rejects the idea of rehabilitating either suitor. Cheril escapes to a Grand Teton cirque lake. There, she meets a bow hunter from Oregon, scouting for bighorn sheep. A valentine arrow pierces her heart when he joins her in fishing with his self-tied Alexandra Streamer. Ever after, they together take big native cutthroat trout.[12]

Fantasy Literature

In our review of classic literature (Chapter 4 above), we looked at paragraphs on fishing from Jules Verne's *20,000 Leagues Under the Sea.* That novel is, essentially, science fiction. A closely related genre would be fantasy literature. A fly-fishing novel that fits such a description is *The Snowfly* by Joseph Heywood, described as

> . . . a page-turner that takes you on a hunt through Vietnam, Soviet Russia, and a vast Canadian wasteland. The holy grail that burns at its core is the snowfly, a legendary insect—enormous, white, and exceedingly rare—that attracts trout of such size that

12. My adult daughters, Melissa White Addington and Cheril White Loper, with whom I shared these plots, say the names should be changed to make the fabrication complete.

> they couldn't possibly exist in the world as we know it. But in *The Snowfly*, such things can and do exist.[13]

In the novel, the protagonist discovers giant mayflies embedded in Jurassic fossil beds. He ties fishing flies with two-foot wingspans to match the fossil flies and then goes worldwide to find a fish, he hopes still extant, that might take his re-creation. Eventually, he goes up a river beyond rivers on the Kamchatka Peninsula, located in far northeast Russia. That peninsula lies between the Sea of Okhotsk and the Bering Sea. The low coastlands of the Kamchatka are crossed by many rivers with extensive swamps. That is where the protagonist casts his snowfly—and catches a trout in excess of 50 inches!

It's hard to imagine casting such a dry fly to such a fish, but, in a fantasy novel, why not? For the average angler with shallow pockets, a fishing trip up the Amazon River for peacock bass or up the Congo in Africa for the giant mbenga would be a sufficient dream—that is, fantasy—come true.

A fantasy novel that deals with civilization-building is *Island in the Sea of Time* by S. M. Stirling. The story begins one spring on Nantucket Island, where everything appears perfectly normal. Suddenly, a storm blankets the entire island. When the weather clears, the island's inhabitants find that they are no longer in the late 20th century but have been transported instead to the Bronze Age! With no electricity or any other modern convenience, the islanders must create their world from scratch. They become, essentially, a hunter-gatherer culture, but, because of their oceanic location, theirs is a fisher-digger culture—digging in the sand for clams and fishing for sea creatures farther from shore. As the story progresses, the islanders must confront would-be conquerors.[14]

A third fishy fantasy tale is Daniel Wallace's *Big Fish: A Novel of Mythic Proportions*. This 1998 book was made into a movie and later into a musical stage play. In the book, we learn that Edward Bloom, the protagonist, is a big fish in a small Alabama town. During all his long years, he tells jokes that keep people at a distance and recants tales about his life that may or may not be true. One such account is of catching a catfish as "big as a man" that, as Edward tells it, pulled him out of his boat and down into the depths of Big Lake. There, he saw the town of his youth, which had been submerged when the reservoir was built. He also spots old friends, who wave at him. Finally, the giant fish—"six or seven feet long"—throws him onto the shore, sans rod and reel. The truth may be that Bloom fell asleep when fishing from

13. The quotation cited comes from an Internet description of the book. The story is based on my listening to the book on BARD.

14. This book was heard on BARD, then appropriated for this telling.

Big Lake's shoreline and a fish—or a town prankster—made off with his bait and pole.[15]

Bloom's son, William, who narrates the story, engages his father in a deathbed conversation, seeking to understand the truth of the man's life. Rather than succeeding, the son gets four quite different predictions of how the father will die—none of them, as it turns out, a match with reality.

Finally, Edward, on the verge of death, persuades William to spirit him out of the hospital and to a river. Once on the riverbank, the old man suddenly becomes fully alive. He walks into the water unescorted. We read,

> All this time, my father was becoming a fish.
>
> I saw him dart this way and that, silvery, brilliant, shining life, and disappear into the darkness of the deep water where the big fish go, and I haven't seen him since the others have. Already I've heard stories, of lives saved and wishes granted, of children carried for miles on his back, anglers mischievously dumped from their vessels and emptied into various oceans and streams from Beaufort to Hyannis by the biggest fish they've ever seen, and they tell their stories to anybody who will listen.
>
> But no one believes them. No one believes a word.[16]

Horror Stories and Movies

For inclusion in this collected works, perhaps to a reader's surprise, come fishing horror stories that go well beyond everyday angler accounts of falling in a stream or losing a rod but may involve creatures from the deep. One such horror story, initially believable, is *The Fisherman* by John Langan, which won the 2016 Bram Stoker Award.

In Langan's novel, two friends, Abe and Dan, both recently widowed, go fishing on Dutchman's Creek in upstate New York. This seldom-fished creek, they are warned, is one on which many people have mysteriously died. Those deaths date back a century to when the reservoir was built and the creek created. At that time, Dort house was on this property, inhabited by a shadowy figure called "The Fisherman." The Fisherman occasionally was spotted in deepening dusk, haunting the shores, casting out line, and measuring it. In the reservoir's construction camp were many European immigrants, including a woman whose son is killed in a freak horse-cart accident. She goes mad and dies. Her husband takes her body to the Dort

15. Wallace, *Big Fish*, 34–36.

16. Wallace, *Big Fish*, 180.

house rather than burying her. From that mysterious house, she eventually returns, yellow-eyed but alive. Also in the camp is a man who, in Germany, had been a professor of philology with a specialty in ancient Egyptian occult manuscripts on Osiris and the underworld. As more deaths occur, the professor goes with village men to storm the mysterious house of the Fisherman. Breaking through the front door, they find themselves on the cold shore of a black ocean. Going out from the shore are heavy, hook-laden lines, placed there by the Fisherman. On one line, he has hooked a monster fish, fearsome and primordial, essentially Leviathan. The huge fish threatens to pull all of them into the deep—and succeeds with the Fisherman. Suddenly, this whale-become-a-mountain turns to attack them. In the melee, one man with a knife hacks a comrade to a bloody death. The remainder flee back to and through the Dort house.

That's the story that Abe and Dan are told regarding their fishing locale. The two friends go fishing on the creek, and Abe, casting into a deep pool, hooks and catches a four-foot catfish or pike or manatee or porpoise or mermaid, who transforms into the glowingly beautiful being of his deceased wife. Reunited, they make love, but then she transforms again, this time into a yellow-eyed, cat-toothed, clawed, water-dripping monster. Abe flees. His partner Dan is, likewise, reunited with his deceased but transformed wife. Dan, however, chooses to stay with her and, in so doing, disappears. Perhaps he drowns. Regardless, his body is never found.

For years thereafter, Abe no longer fishes on Dutchman Creek. One rainy spring, however, the creek behind his house overflows, making a lake of his backyard. Out of that lake, inviting Abe to join him, is his old friend Dan, along with hundreds of slimy creatures (including his wife and Dan's) and the Fisherman—all are yellow-eyed with their heads poking out just above the water. Abe declines the invitation to go with them. Then, the water recedes, and the creatures slip away, at least, temporarily.

Perhaps scarier is *Creature From the Black Lagoon,* which was presented first as a 1954 black-and-white Hollywood movie and later novelized. The story is not about fishing for denizens of the deep but about denizen zombies of the swamp going after humans. In the film, a 200,000-year-old fossil with webbed fingers is found in the Amazon. An expedition is organized, leading scientists deep into Brazilian swampy water, the Black Lagoon. Two of the men in the party are killed, savaged by a wild beast that disappears. In one extended scene, to pleasant Henry Mancini music, the beautiful ichthyologist Kay Lawrence, played by Julie Adams, goes for a long, languid swim. Suddenly, the music turns dark, as a being with a sharp spine and webbed hands and feet begins to swim underneath her. The audience screams; the creature reaches for her ankle.

Another watery horror story is *The Horror of Party Beach*, a terrible spoof of beach-party movies. The film takes place on the coast of Connecticut, not California. Like *Black Lagoon*, *Beach Party*, too, is a black-and-white, low-budget film, but this one comes complete with beach music, bikini-clad girls, muscled guys, twist dancing, a motorcycle gang, and fistfights—up until someone says, "Something smells fishy." Then, from slimy polluted water comes a gilled mutant with eyes like ping-pong balls who is hungry for teenage blood. After lots of on-screen screams and a couple more "something smells fishy" scenes with attendant blood sucking, the monster is finally driven back to the sea. One critic says that this movie is "one of the worst of all time."

Chapter 7

Informational and Instructive Treatises

A seventh distinct genre of fishing literature is informational and instructive contributions—where-to-, how-to-, and with-what-to-fish accounts. Such will be found in journals, manuals, books, and stand-alone essays, such are found on the Internet. Often enough, they are stories in themselves or are embedded in angling tales. They exist in abundance, publishers knowing that fishers are more interested in improving their knowledge and skills—so that they can catch more fish—than in reading another predictable "Me and Joe Went A-fishing" report.

The written evidence that this genre stands in ancient tradition comes down to us from the Roman Claudius Aelian (170–234 C.E.). With fly and equipment descriptions and imaginative entry into the piscine mind, he describes the angling practice of Macedonian fishermen on the Astraeus River:

> They fasten red wool . . . round a hook and fit on to the wool two feathers which grow under a cock's wattles, and which in color are like wax. Their rod is six feet long, and their line is the same length. Then they throw their snare, and the fish, attracted and maddened by the color, comes straight at it, thinking from the pretty sight to gain a dainty mouthful; when, however, it opens its jaws, it is caught by the hook, and enjoys a bitter repast, a captive.[1]

Aelian also reports words of an earlier Roman poet, Marcus Valerius Martialis, aka Martial, (38–104 C.E.). Martial is best remembered for pithy epigrams. One line from his observations—though it may not be his but that of an author unknown—could be the oldest clear reference to fly fishing that exists:

> Who has not seen the scarus rise,

1. Brooks, *Trout Fishing*, 2.

Decoyed, and fooled by fraudful flies?[2]

As to what "scarus" are, they could be in the parrotfish family or, just possibly, trout. "Fraudful" may be a synonym for "artificial" although there are other interpretations of the word in this context. Still, the line may well mean, "Who has not seen trout rise, decoyed, and fooled by artificial flies?"

Martial also has a poem in which he extols the pleasure of fishing with its escape from city life in Rome and gives information on fish:

Not far the fisher needs to roam,
But in the waters clear and still
Beneath the casement of his home
May watch and take his prey at will;
And here though Aeolus should rave,
The table lacks not dainty fare;
The fish-pool fears no angry wave,
Pike, mullet, lampreys all are there,
Home-bred its denizens and tame
Huge mullets here and barbel swim,
Whose keeper knows them all by name
And at his call they come to him.[3]

If he could, Martial might give us a good fishing tale of angling on the Upper Tiber, where, in 2015, my daughter Melissa and I took brown trout and grayling.

Earlier than Martial was Pūblius Ovidius Nāsō, known in English as Ovid (43 B.C.E.–18 C.E.). He is well-remembered for two classic books: *The Metamorphoses* and *The Art of Love.* Another book, *Halieutica*, has been attributed to him although it probably was penned well after Ovid's time. Regardless of authorship, counsel on angling is given in it, for example, "Let your hook be always cast; in the pool where you least expect it, there will be a fish." In addition, *Halieutica* classifies fish caught, relying on Aristotle's centuries-earlier taxonomy. Most interesting, the author compares fishing to writing. Fishing becomes, in the *Halieutica,* analogous to the art of writing. The chief weapon of the angler, the fishing pole, is "harundo" in Latin, but the word also means "reed," the tool by which ancient writers penned

2. Angling author Joe Brooks says that William Radcliff in 1921 held that this statement belonged to Martial. While reading several hundred of Martial's epigrams, I never found it. Nor could Dr. Carol Neel, classics historian at Colorado College, locate it. Brooks and Ratcliff, then, could be wrong. At best, we can say, "It's old . . . and probably Roman."

3. Martialis, *Twelve Books of Epigrams*, bk 10, p. 309.

their works. In addition, angling and writing, says the author of *Halieutica*, both involve deception to lure and catch the quarry, be that fish or reader.

As noted in Chapter 1 of this book, the great Greek philosopher Aristotle (383–322 B.C.E.) was "the first ichthyologist." How he became such is a fish tale in itself. Aristotle came to Athens from Macedonia to study at Plato's Academy. He was there for 20 years. When a new and anti-Macedonian ruler took over Athens, Aristotle was forced to leave the city for the Isle of Lesbos. Here, he began serious investigation of that island's flora and fauna, including fish species of freshwater ponds and of saltwater harbors. His observations on the anatomy of octopus, cuttlefish, crustaceans, and many other marine invertebrates were remarkably accurate. And, though he understandably misidentified whales and dolphins as fish rather than mammals, he got it right that sharks give live birth to their young. As an islander and an ichthyologist, Aristotle likely caught fish himself—at the very least, he must have received them—and then examined, dissected, and classified his take, eventually organizing them into 54 categories.[4] His island research was held as the gospel truth well into the Middle Ages.

Mention of fishing occurs earlier than Aristotle and in the wider world beyond Athens and Rome. From Egyptian hieroglyphics, we learn that ancient folk were fishing in 3100 B.C.E. That is a thousand years earlier than *The Epic of Gilgamesh*, with which this book began.[5] The Egyptians angled from the banks of the Nile and in boats and rafts made from papyrus and other reeds. They used a variety of techniques, including baited hooks, hand nets, dragnets, fish baskets or weir traps, and harpoons. Hooks were carved from pieces of bone, wood, shell, or ivory. Such hooks were recently discovered deep in the mud along the Jordan River in Israel, dating back 12,000 to 14,000 years! They were used to catch carp—or the carp's ancestor—and, evidence suggests, those hooks could have been dressed artificially.[6]

We can go back even further. In his angling book *The Unreasonable Virtue of Fly Fishing*, Mark Kurlansky indicates that how-to knowledge has

4. Today, fish are grouped by domain, kingdom, phylum, class, order, family, genus, and species—over 29,000 in arrangement, they being the most diverse group of vertebrates on Earth. To identify all these species, fish with similar external anatomy features or traits are grouped into families. For example, fish in the pike family have a long, slender body and sharp teeth.

5. See ch. 1, which relates this 2100 B.C.E. Babylonian legend.

6. Pindyck, "Ancient Carping," 32.

been around a long time. He says that 70,000 years ago, before hooks were employed, people caught fish with gorges, a gorge being

> . . . a piece of flint, bone, shell, or horn, pointed on both ends. Very early humans knew how to entice the fish to swallow the gorge . . . by putting bait on it. When the line was pulled tight, the gorge turned sideways in the fish's throat. Gorges that are seventy thousand years old, from the Paleolithic period, have been found.[7]

Skipping forward, Kurlansky notes that the Maori made hooks from human bones, the people of New Guinea from insect claws. Hooks also were fashioned from eagle jaws and cactus spurs. The Chinese, he says, were already using artificial flies 3,500 years ago.

Returning the reader to the Greco-Roman world, Kurlansky notes that Plutarch (46 C.E.–119 C.E.) recommended braided horsehair for fishing line—preferably from a white stallion, such being stronger than the mane or tail of other horses, he claimed. When Kurlansky considers fishing in 17th-century England, he notes that one writer from that time suggested making bait from powdered human skulls obtained by robbing graves![8]

After the fifth century C.E. and for the next 900 years, there is little written on fishing generally, much less fly fishing, that is informational or instructive. Even so, we may be sure that people went to water with a rod, net, or spear in hand. The saintly stories in Chapter 3, lifting up Brendan of Ireland, Saint Corentin in France, and Brother Anthony of Padua, vouchsafe that people were close to water, interacted thereon, and likely knew how to get fish there.

During the Middle Ages, Europe was an Eastern Orthodox and Roman Catholic world, pious in the main and rules-observant. The church held that eating red meat should not happen on Fridays (the day Christ died). Fish, though, was not considered meat and so became the staple food of the believer's diet on designated days. Such a diet was provided by serious fishing. Just how big an enterprise fishing was is suggested in the article "The International Fishery of the 16th Century." What was true in that century would hold for those earlier. That report says:

7. Kurlansky, *Unreasonable Virtue of Fly Fishing* (2021), 62. Some information by Kurlansky, shared below, first came to my attention in the March 20, 2021, *Wall Street Journal* article "Life on the Fly" by Bill Heavey.

8. Kurlansky, *Unreasonable Virtue of Fly Fishing* (2021).

> More Europeans at the end of the 15th century were engaged in fishing than in any other occupation except farming. This fact reflects the importance that fish played in the everyday diet of Europeans. It was a source of protein that was easy to preserve, transport, purchase and prepare. Moreover, in an age of rising (and warring) nation-states, fish made an ideal military ration.[9]

In addition to fish from the sea, there were those taken from lakes, rivers, and streams. They were caught in myriad ways: wicker traps, thread nets, pond draining, and sharpened hooks. Some of those hooks surely were dressed with feather, fur, and "red cloth"—a la the Macedonian angler of the first century.

Let us now leave the Late Middle Ages to a time closer to our own, when fly fishing as we know it is recognizable and comes with clearer instructions on angling.

In the late 15th century came a fly-fishing writer with instructional accounts for salmonoid fishers. She is Dame Juliana Berners, prioress of the Sopwell Nunnery near London. She writes *A Treatyse of Fysshynge Wyth an Angle.* In the year 1496, it was published in *The Book of Saint Alban.* Her informational, instructive, and technical work is often used to date the birth of sportfishing. The dame deserves to be crowned "The Mother of Fly Fishing," having written 150 years prior to "Our Father" Izaak Walton, whose work was considered in Chapter 4.

Translated into modern English, here is a sample of Dame Juliana's advice:

> If you would be skilled in angling, you must first learn how to make your tackle: that is to say, your rod, and your lines of various colors. After that you must know how to angle; in what part of the water, how deep, at what time of day, for what kind of fish, in what weather; how many obstacles there are to this kind of fishing called angling, and especially what bait to use for each kind of fish in every month of the year; also how to make your baits breed, where you shall find them and how you shall keep them; and the most skilled art of all, how to make your hooks, of steel or of osmund, some to be dubbed and some for the float

9. "The International Fishery of the 16th Century" with excellent maps is found on the Newfoundland and Labrador Heritage website.

> and the ground bait. You shall hereafter find all these things expressed openly to your knowledge.[10]

Here are her recipes for the flies to be used in the month of May:

> The yellow fly. The body of yellow wool: the wings of the red cocks hackle and of the drake dyed yellow. The black leaper. The body of black wool and lapped about with the herl of the peacock tail: and the wings of the red capon with a blue head.[11]

She ends her treatise with these words:

> All those who keep these rules shall have the blessing of God and of St. Peter, which blessing may He grant to them, Who has redeemed us with His Precious Blood.[12]

Dame Juliana Berners Demonstrates Her Fishing Technique

Since Dame Juliana's time, countless others have shared fly-fishing knowledge in book form. Holly Morris, as quoted in the foreword of this book, estimates that more than 5,000 fly-fishing books can be found in the English language. The majority, I am convinced, are of the practical variety

10. Berners, *Treatyse.*
11. Berners, *Treatyse.*
12. Berners, *Treatyse.*

although, often enough, the fishing advice includes a story, such as "how I developed the X-fly pattern" or "the summer that I discovered Hidden Lake." Lots of the books cover fly patterns and tying techniques. My personal bookshelf has more than a hundred offerings to improve my fishing. A few years ago, I asked a number of angling friends to share what have been the most influential, informative, enjoyable, helpful—even inspirational—fishing books for them.[13] Most colleagues, after naming *A River Runs Through It*, mentioned authors and titles helpful in becoming a better fisher, especially John Gierach, whose books we shall attend to in Chapter 12. Some of these authors and their books are listed below; many of these authors have additional offerings. Here, then, is a list of angling favorites:

American Fly-Fishing Trade Association, *Fly-Fishing Tactics*

Paul Arnold, *Wisdom of the Guides*

John Barr, *Barr Flies*

Joseph D. Bates Jr., *Trout Waters and How To Fish Them*

Robert Behnke, *Trout and Salmon of North America*

Ray Bergman, *Trout*

A. K. Best, *Fly Fishing With A. K.*

Gary Borger, *Nymphing: A Basic Guide*

Charles E. Brooks, *Fishing Yellowstone Waters*

Joe Brooks, *Trout Fishing*

Charlie Craven, *Basic Fly-Tying*

Jack Dennis, *Western Trout Fly Tying Manual*

Kirk Dieter and Charlie Meyers, *Little Red Book of Fly Fishing*

Pat Dorsey, *Fly Fishing Tailwaters: Tactics*

Ed Engle, *Splitting Cain: Conversations With Bamboo Rod Makers*

Doug Fisher and Carl Richards, *Selective Trout*

Art Flick, *Streamside Guide to Naturals and Their Imitations*

Paul N. Fling and Donald L. Puterbaugh, *The Basic Manual of Fly-Tying*

13. With thanks to the following colleagues who offered titles of their favorite books: Rick Bailey, Andy Blackman, Alan Conger, Ron Dunn, Mike Emerson, Guy Fredella, Henry Hughes, Bruce Kuster, Neil Luehring, Mark Mahler, Jody Martin, Cat O'Grady, Reuben Rainey, Rick Shick, John Stefonik, Anthony Surage, Greg Walters, Michelle White, Jim Williams, and members of the Pikes Peak Chapter of Trout Unlimited and Pikes Peak Fly Fishers, Colorado Springs.

Ira N. Gabrielson, editor, *The Fisherman's Encyclopedia*

John Gierach, *Good Flies*

Arnold Gingrich, *The Well-tempered Angler*

Theodore Gordon, *American Trout Fishing*

Harry Plunkett Green, *Where the Bright Waters Meet*

Josh Greenberg, *Trout Water*

Roderick Haig-Brown, *To Know a River*

F. M. Halford, *Dry-Fly Fishing*

George Harvey, *Memories, Patterns and Tactics*

Edward R. Hewitt, *A Trout and Salmon Fisherman for 75 Years*

Roger Hill, *Fishing the South Platte River*

John Waller Hills, *A History of Fly Fishing for Trout*

Dan Holland, *The Trout Fisherman's Bible*

Herbert Hoover, *Fishing for Fun*

Dave Hughes, *Trout Rigs and Methods*

Henry Hughes, *Back Seat With Fish: A Man's Adventures in Angling and Romance*

Preston J. Jennings, *A Book of Trout Flies*

John Judy, *Slack Line, Strategies for Fly Fishing*

Nick Karas, *Brook Trout*

Lefty Kreh, *Presenting the Fly*

Karel Krivanec, *Czech Nymph and Other Related Fly Fishing Methods*

Mark Kurlansky, *Cod: A Biography of the Fish That Changed the World*

Jerry Kustich, *A Wisp in the Wind*

George M. L. LaBranche, *The Dry Fly and Fast Water*

Gary LaFontaine, *Caddis Flies*

Ted Leeson, *The Habit of Rivers*

Nick Lyons, *Bright Rivers*

Mary Orvis Marbury, *Favorite Flies and Their Histories*

Vincent C. Marinaro, *A Modern Dry-Fly Code*

Landon Mayer, *How To Catch the Biggest Trout of Your Life*

A. J. McClane, *The Wise Fishermen's Encyclopedia*
Tom McNally, *The Complete Book of Fly Fishing*
Matthew Miller, *Fishing Through the Apocalypse*
Ray Ovington, *Tactics on Trout*
Datus C. Proper, *What the Trout Said*
James Prosek, *Trout of the World*
Steve Raymond, *Nervous Water*
Duane Redford, *Fly Fisher's Playbook*
Barrie Rickards, *Freshwater Fishing*
Charles Ritz, *A Fly Fisher's Life*
R. H. Russell, *The Speckled Brook Trout*
Paul Schullery, *Cowboy Trout: Western Fly Fishing As If It Matters*
Ernest Schweibert, *Matching the Hatch and Death of a Riverkeeper*
Jack Shaw, *Flyfish the Trout Lakes*
G. E. M. Skues, *Minor Tactics of the Chalk Stream*
W. C. Stewart, *The Practical Angler*
Doug Swisher and Carl Richard, *Selective Trout*
Robert Traver, *Trout Madness*
Patrick Trotter, *Cutthroat: Native Trout of the West*
Larry Tullis, *Nymphing Strategies*
C. F. Walker, *The Art of Chalk Stream Fishing*
Isaak Walton and Charles Cotton, *The Compleat Angler*
Charles F. Waterman, *Mist on the River: Remembrances of Dan Bailey*
Frank D. Weissbarth, *Holy Ghost Creek*
Henry P. Wells, *Fly-Rods and Fly Tackle*
Michele White, *Joe Schmo Can Catch a Big Fish*
Dave Whitlock, *Trout and Their Food: A Complete Guide for Fishers*
Joan Wulff, *New Fly-fishing Techniques*
Lee Wulff, *Bush Pilot Angler*

The Prosek, Behnke, and Whitlock volumes carry exquisite watercolors. Other instructive-informational books are well-illustrated with photographs and drawings. There are many other titles that could be added to those above. Of the innumerable books about fishing, the greatest number are decidedly of the informational variety.

Charlie Brooks' writings are exemplary where-to fishing literature. In his classic *Fishing Yellowstone Waters*, he takes the reader with him to the rivers of the national park, even describing various holes and runs. Here's what he says about the Firehole:

> The Firehole rises in tiny Madison Lake, which lies in a marshy subalpine basin at 8,200 feet along a north-facing slope of the continental divide. From the lake to the bridge on the Old Faithful-Thumb road under which it passes, this is a tiny, cold, winding brook trout stream that also holds a few pan-size brookies.[14]

What he says, I can absolutely attest to, having fished that stretch per his instructions. About the Lamar River, Brooks writes,

> For reasons not yet explained, the cutthroat migrates or roves about, upstream and down. This will cause puzzlement among anglers; the riffle or run that produced well this week may appear as barren as a snowbank the next week. The answer, for the angler, is to move up or down and try to locate where the fish are holding at this time.[15]

Illustrative of how-to material is *Czech Nymph* by Karel Krivanec, whose "nymphing school" I attended on the Vltava River in the Czech Republic. He instructs as follows:

> At first glance, the basic procedure in short nymphing seems very easy. Using a suitable rod, we prepare to fish our two or three nymphs with, at most, 50–150 cm of fly line and the leader outside the top guide. We will choose the most suitable place for fishing at the edge of the current, possibly on the bank of a deep stream, or pool. Then, standing sideways on—i.e. at right angles—to the current, we use a flip of the wrist, and an underhand pendulum swing to lob the nymphs a short distance upstream. Once the nymphs have reached the riverbed, we lift the rod tip with our casting arm approximately parallel to the water. This leaves a short piece of fly line and a longer section of leader descending vertically into the water immediately below the rod tip.

14. Brooks, *Fishing Yellowstone Waters*, 53.
15. Brooks, *Fishing Yellowstone Waters*, 37.

> The extent to which we lift line from the water depends on the water depth and the length of the leader. From this moment and with our casting arm extended at full stretch, we utilize the rod tip to lead the nymphs downstream with slightly positive drag. The balance achieved with the special leader and the weighted nymphs provides a sensitive, tactile, and visual link between rod hand, rod tip and flies. It is essential not to move the flies too quickly. They must be drawn gently and delicately downstream using a combination of arm movement and a lifting of the rod tip so that the speed at which the line/leader combination is moving is slightly slower than that of the surface current. Achieving optimal drift speed is the key to success with this method.[16]

Detailed information, such as the above, is regularly given in the where-to-fish and how-to-fish literature. The American Fly-Fishing Trade Association book *Fly-Fishing Tactics* includes a comprehensive section on everything from assembling your tackle, best flies and knots, to wind casting.

Before leaving this chapter, mention must be made of Paul Schullery's *Cowboy Trout: Western Fly Fishing As If It Matters*. The stories in this book, compiled by the long-time curator of the Western Museum of Fly Fishing, speak of fly fishing broadly but especially focus on angling in Montana around Yellowstone. Included are writings by Edward Hewitt, George Grant, Norman "Bunyonbug" Means, Bud Lilly, Dan Bailey, Ted Trueblood (of *Field and Stream*), Art Flick, and others. If you want the full story of the "salmon fly" (*Pteronarcys californica*), for instance, and its imitations (e.g., "the sofa pillow"), this is the book to read. Here is an illustrative section discussing flies and involving the well-known English poet-angler Rudyard Kipling. Schullery says,

> Western fly fishing stopped being a pioneer adventure soon after there were stagecoaches and trains stopping regularly in the neighborhood. As far as western preferences for fly patterns, my own impression from reading great amounts of this 19th century material is that by the 1880s at least some western anglers, whether resident or tourist, actually concluded that muted colors worked best. That certainly was the opinion of at least one visitor, Rudyard Kipling, after fishing Wyoming and Colorado and talking with local fishermen in 1889:"If ever any man works the western trout streams, he would do well to bring out with him the dingiest flies he possesses. The natives laugh at the tiny English hooks, but they hold, and duns and drabs and sober

16. Krivanec et al., *Czech Nymph*, 29.

grays seem to tickle the aesthetic taste of the trout." Kipling seems to have encountered the salmon fly himself, judging from the near-raving excitement of his account of fishing Yankee Jim Canyon on the Yellowstone River, where he found the water willow crowded with the breeding trout fly in early July. Obviously, some people, the natives he mentioned, disagreed over fly pattern or hook size but they knew what worked for them too.[17]

In this genre, the reader may have sensed the full weight of a little "feather and fluff" on wire ever so light. For fishers, it is seldom as simple as, "You get a line and I'll get a pole; honey, baby mine." No, things are often more complicated—at times, esoteric—like, "In this tailwater release when the cfs is less than 50, with a 10-foot 2-weight rod, you'll want to put a #24 red zebra midge with 1.5 millimeter tungsten bead head on a 9-foot 5-x tapered leader and 6x fluorocarbon tippet fished without indicator, high-sticked, tight-lined and moved with the current."

Fishing guides and everyday anglers often encase a shorter story in a fishing report. Hundreds—no, thousands—of sites exist on the Internet, two sources are midcurrent.com/news and news.orvis.com/fly-fishing. In addition, an Internet search on "fly fishing bloggers" will yield a long list of sites. Some sites have videos with demonstrations that are sometimes stories in themselves.

Annually, Maine, New Jersey, Pennsylvania, Georgia, Colorado, and California each host a fly-fishing show, featuring products for sale, travel offerings, talks by pros, movies, fly-tying demonstrations, and more. Often enough, attendees will hear and meet the authors whose tales they've read in various publications.

17. Schullery, *Cowboy Trout*, 132–33.

Chapter 8

Nursery Rhymes and Children's Stories

The previous chapter, dealing with the where-to and how-to of angling matters, took us deeply into the world of fly fishing itself. Let us now move to children's literature having to do with fish, angling, and water. Such includes nursery rhymes, bedtime stories, and books that children could enjoy alone but often enjoy with loved ones.

Let me begin, though, with a caveat by British journalist Malcolm Muggeridge:

> Children's books are probably the most difficult of all to write; they are certainly the most difficult to review. For children alone can properly judge their worth, and children, very wisely, never review. An adult has to refer back to his own childhood and ask himself: Would I have enjoyed such a book then?[1]

For the children's books, rhymes, and tales treated in this chapter, the answer to that question is a resounding, "Yes, I would have thoroughly enjoyed them."

I start with a little rhyme with which I grew up:

Fishy, fishy in the brook,
Daddy catch you on a hook,
Momma fry you in a pan,
Jimmy eats you as fast as he can.

That is my earliest-heard nursery rhyme, but here is another that many a youngster knows:

Dance to your daddy,

1. Muggeridge, "Swallows and Amazons Book Review."

My little laddie.
Dance to your daddy, my little man.
You shall have a fishy
In a little dishy.
You shall have a fishy when the boat comes in.

For gender inclusivity, "laddie" can become "lassie" and "man" changed to "one."

And let us not forget:

Rub-a-dub-dub,
Three men in a tub,
And who do you think they be?
The butcher, the baker,
The candlestick-maker,
All put out to sea.

Another fishy rhyme, not so well known but still delightful, is this one from *The Oxford Dictionary of Nursery Rhymes*:

One, two, three, four, five,
Once I caught a fish alive,
Six, seven, eight, nine, ten,
Then I let it go again.

Why did you let it go?
Because it bit my finger so.
Which finger did it bite?
This little finger on the right.[2]

Well-known and sung with delight by children is the rhyme about "Baby Beluga," a little white whale who swims and splashes all day in the deep blue sea.[3]

Another nursery rhyme with which most youngsters are familiar is Eugene Field's classic. The poem is a bedtime story about three children sailing and fishing among the stars.

Wynken, Blynken, and Nod one night
Sailed off in a wooden shoe—
Sailed on a river of crystal light
Into a sea of dew.
"Where are you going, and what do you wish?"
The old moon asked the three.

2. Opie and Opie, *Oxford Dictionary of Nursery Rhymes*, 334.

3. Cavoukian, *Baby Beluga*.

"We have come to fish for the herring-fish
That live in this beautiful sea;
Nets of silver and gold have we,"
Said Wynken, Blynken, and Nod.

What a wonderful way to go to sleep—with visions of twinkling waves, shining stars, and herring in one's head!

Wynken, Blynken, and Nod Sailing Off in a Wooden Shoe

For many English-speaking children, one of the earliest books read to them is Dr. Seuss' classic *One Fish Two Fish Red Fish Blue Fish*. The book contains colorful and imaginative art, and, after beginning with the titular line, the rhyming continues as follows:

Black fish blue fish old fish new fish
This one has a little star.
This one has a little car.
Say! What a lot of fish there are.[4]

Andrew Stanton's story *Finding Nemo*, converted into a Walt Disney animated movie, tells of an overly cautious clown fish named Marlin, who loses his son, Nemo, to a pair of human divers. Marlin then begins a search

4. Dr. Seuss, *One Fish Two Fish*, 2–3.

for the lost child. On his way, he meets a blue reef fish named Dory, who then accompanies Marlin on his journey to find Nemo. En route, they encounter a storm of jellyfish as well as surfing sea turtles—among other sea creatures and many dangers. Meanwhile, as his father and Dory search, Nemo, held captive in the fish tank of a dentist's office, plots his own escape. At the film's end, all are happily reunited.

The most richly colorful children's book involving the catch of fish is David Shannon's *Jangles: A BIG Fish Story*. As the tale goes, a father—named "Dad"— and his son are seated on a riverbank, a green tackle box between them. Dad tells the boy about a fish called Jangles:

> When I was a kid, Jangles was the biggest fish anyone had ever seen—or heard! That's right, you could hear Jangles. He'd broken so many fishing lines that his huge, crooked jaw was covered with shiny metal lures and rusty old fishhooks of all shapes and sizes. They clinked and clattered as he swam. That's why he was called Jangles.[5]

Dad says that he finally caught this fish and, by it, was transported to the bottom of the deep. There, Jangles told him stories dating from the beginning of time. So, instead of taking the fish home for dinner, Dad freed Jangles after removing all the jangling lures. Dad provides evidence of the truth of his tale when he opens his green tackle box to show his son that it is full to the top with shiny metal lures and rusty old fishhooks of all shapes and sizes. After all, what else could explain the presence of those lures and hooks!

Margaret Wise Brown, author of the ever-so-loved *Goodnight Moon*, also penned *The Fish With the Deep Sea Smile*. Beautifully illustrated, here are the opening lines:

> They fished and they fished
> Way down in the sea,
> Down in the sea a mile.
> They fished among all the fish in the sea,
> For the fish with the deep sea smile.[6]

5. Shannon, *Jangles*, 2. The publisher of *Jangles* describes the book thus: "David Shannon instantly hooks [no pun intended?] readers with this stunning, highly entertaining tour-de-force—his best book ever! Breathtaking oil paintings bursting with energy pull readers along into Big Lake, the home of Jangles, the biggest fish anyone has seen." A musical version of this story, called "Old Whiskers," is reviewed in the "Gone Fishin' Songs" chapter of this book.

6. Brown, *Fish With the Deep Sea Smile*, 1–4.

They caught a fish with blue-green eyes and whiskers three, another with electric lights, and still others with a variety of strange and wonderful features.

> And then one day they got a pull,
> From down in the sea a mile.
> And when they pulled the fish into the boat,
> He smiled a DEEP SEA SMILE.
>
> And as he smiled the hook got free,
> And then, what a deep sea smile!
> He flipped his tail and swam away,
> Down in the sea a mile.[7]

A happy ending for the deep-sea fish and young readers, leaving all smiling and, perhaps, providing an argument for catch-and-release angling.

A most beloved story of the mystical sea and its creatures is Hans Christian Andersen's *The Little Mermaid*. In that story, the Little Mermaid—half-human, half-fish—rescues a prince from drowning when his ship is wrecked. She takes him to a temple onshore. He falls in love with her and she with him. She even is willing to exchange her tail for legs. However, in that same temple, an equally beautiful human princess dwells. The prince mistakenly thinks that she is his rescuer. So, he falls in love with her, and they marry, much to the heartbreak of the Little Mermaid. The newlyweds' honeymoon is aboard a ship, and the Little Mermaid is tempted by sister mermaids to kill the prince with a knife but doesn't. After 300 years, the angels take her to heaven, away from mermaid-mandated death in the sea. As "a daughter of the air," she lives forever in heaven and forever in the hearts of children.[8]

Another beloved children's story involving fish is *The Adventures of Pinocchio*, written in 1883 by Italian Carlo Collodi. As the story is told, Pinocchio, a wooden puppet, dreams of becoming a real boy. However, as a result of disobedience and many misadventures, Pinocchio and his maker, Geppetto, become separated. Geppetto boards a small boat to search for the boy, but the boat is overturned by a giant dogfish—or, in another version, a

7. Brown, *Fish With the Deep Sea Smile*, 19–24.

8. In the Copenhagen harbor is a statue of Andersen's Little Mermaid, showing her becoming human. This waterside icon, unveiled in 1913, has been defaced, stolen, and damaged through the years, then returned, rescued, and restored, making for a story in itself.

whale, or, in a third, a terrible shark—and Geppetto and boat are swallowed by the fish. In time, Pinocchio goes in search of his father and, led by a friendly dolphin—or a tuna, depending on the version read—he is taken into the monster-fish's mouth and down to its stomach. There, he finds Geppetto on his boat, trapped and near-starvation (provisions from a consumed merchant ship having been exhausted after two years). He had been fishing without luck, but, suddenly, the monster-fish opens its mouth, and, in the movie version of this tale, water pours in as well as fish after fish. Geppetto and Pinocchio now cast out and haul in one big fish after another, more than enough to feed them, saving their lives until they can escape from the monster. In one version of the tale, Geppetto and Pinocchio escape by tickling the roof of the fish's mouth so that the monster sneezes them out. In another version, the two start a smoky fire and are coughed onto land. In a third, they sneak out when the gigantic fish is snoring. In most versions, the two are cast into the sea to be rescued by the friendly dolphin—or tuna. That fish swims them back to land, and the adventures of Pinocchio carry on landward from there.[9]

Although starting on the written page, *Pinocchio*, *The Little Mermaid*, and *Finding Nemo* all came to life in Walt Disney animated movies. A silver-screen fish story also was told in another Disney film, the 1940 movie *Fantasia* (re-released in theaters in 1963 and remastered into *Fantasia 2000* in 1999). To the orchestral music of Ottorino Respighi's *Pines of Rome*, the moviegoer follows a baby beluga whale swimming in icy blue Arctic water. When a glacier collapses on the little fellow, he is trapped, forcing him to struggle mightily to find his mother and father. Eventually, he succeeds, and, at the end, the family joins a huge whale pod to swim toward the transcendent northern lights, accompanied by heavenly music.

Elementary-school children may have read Rudyard Kipling's 1902 *Just So Stories for Children*. It carries the account of

"How the Whale Got His Throat"
aka
"The Stute Fish Story"
aka
"The Man of Infinite Resource and Sagacity"
aka
"Latitude Fifty North and Longitude Forty West"
aka
"The Relevance of Suspenders"

9. Collodi, *Pinocchio*, 137–70.

. . . which is just to indicate that this is a complex, yet altogether delightful, tale. Here is my most abbreviated version:

> In the sea, once upon a time, oh my best beloved, a whale ate up all the fish in all the waters of the world—except for one tiny Stute Fish that hid behind the right ear of the whale. The clever Stute Fish tells the whale how tasty human beings can be, persuading the whale to go to latitude fifty north and longitude forty west (England roughly) and, there, swallow a mariner of infinite resources and sagacity, floating on a wooden raft. The man has a jackknife and wears suspenders. "Don't forget about the suspenders," Kipling stresses. So, the whale travels to latitude fifty north and longitude forty west and swallows the tasty, though "nubbly," man of infinite resources and sagacity. Swallowed, the man makes such a row in the whale's dark stomach that the whale takes him home to the white cliffs of Albion. Before the man has landed, however, he uses his jackknife to make a fence from the planks of his raft, which he ties together with his suspenders—"Don't forget about the suspenders"—and positions a fence permanently in the whale's throat, singing,
>
> By means of a grating
> I have stopped your 'ating.
>
> Thereafter, the giant whale cannot eat anything but tiny fish—and krill of course.[10]

Such a tale for a whale, thanks to Rudyard Kipling.

Another greatly loved and widely read children's book meriting mention in this collection is Kenneth Grahame's *The Wind in the Willows*. In this classic, Mole awakens in the springtime from his earthy burrow and makes his way to the riverbank to meet with water-oriented Rat. Rat invites Mole to scull down the river with him in his boat, bringing about this lovely conversation:

> "I beg your pardon," said the Mole, pulling himself together with an effort. "You must think me very rude; but all this is so new to me. So—this—is—a—River!"
>
> "The River," corrected the Rat.
>
> "And you really live by the River? What a jolly life!"

10. Kipling, *Just So Stories for Children*. This story was constructed from my listening to the book on BARD.

> "By it and with it and on it and in it," said the Rat. "It's brother and sister to me, and aunts, and company, and food and drink, and (naturally) washing. It's my world, and I don't want any other. What it hasn't got is not worth having, and what it doesn't know is not worth knowing. Lord! The times we've had together! Whether in winter or summer, spring or autumn, it's always got its fun and its excitements."[11]

As Mole and Rat travel, they meet Otter, who becomes a close friend. Upon leaving the river, Mole and Rat become acquainted with a rich, speedster-driving Toad. In the Wild Wood, they also meet up with wise but reclusive Badger and also encounter rabbits, hedgehogs, field mice, and a horse. Eventually, Mole and Rat winter in Rat's riverside home.

The second year of journeying begins with river activities:

> It was a bright morning in the early part of summer; the river had resumed its wonted banks and its accustomed pace, and a hot sun seemed to be pulling everything green and bushy and spiky up out of the earth towards him, as if by strings. The Mole and the Water Rat had been up since dawn, very busy on matters connected with boats and the opening of the boating season; painting and varnishing, mending paddles, repairing cushions, hunting for missing boat-hooks, and so on.[12]

By the way, the "boat-hooks" mentioned are attached to poles and used for pulling a boat and not for fishing.

The most "watery" chapter in the book is the seventh, "The Piper at the Dawn of Day." It seems that Otter's son, little Portly, wandered away and could not be found. Otter hopes the boy will find his way back to the ford, where he taught the lad to swim and fish. There, he waits, but Portly does not return. That evening, Mole and Rat joined the search in their boat. Drawn by distant, melodious piping all through the night, they scull up a long backwater. The music leads them past a great weir with strong eddies and, finally, to an island. Just as the dawn breaks ever so gloriously, they find Portly. He is asleep between the legs of the large creature that had been doing the piping. The musician may be a cow rather than a divine being, but, in any case, Mole and Rat bow to the creature in gratitude and then row Portly toward home.

11. Grahame, *Wind in the Willows*, ch. 1, "The River Bank." The book was heard on BARD.

12. Grahame, *Wind in the Willows*, ch. 7, "The Piper at the Gates of Dawn." The book was heard on BARD.

> The main river reached again, they turned the boat's head upstream, towards the point where they knew their friend was keeping his lonely vigil. As they drew near the familiar ford, the Mole took the boat in to the bank, and they lifted Portly out and set him on his legs on the tow-path, gave him his marching orders and a friendly farewell pat on the back, and shoved out into mid-stream. They watched the little animal as he waddled along the path contentedly and with importance; watched him till they saw his muzzle suddenly lift and his waddle break into a clumsy amble as he quickened his pace with shrill whines and wriggles of recognition. Looking up the river, they could see Otter start up, tense and rigid, from out of the shallows where he crouched in dumb patience, and could hear his amazed and joyous bark as he bounded up through the osiers on to the path. Then the Mole, with a strong pull on one oar, swung the boat round and let the full stream bear them down again whither it would, their quest now happily ended.[13]

At *The Wind in the Willows*' end, the main characters—Mole, Rat, Toad, Badger, and Otter—picnic together on the riverbank, perhaps enjoying a meal of fresh-caught fish.

Arthur Ransom's *Swallows and Amazons* is the first in a series of children's adventure books of the same name. The series begins with a tale of two families who are on holiday in England's Lake District in 1929. The children of the Walker family—John, Susan, Titty, and Roger—sail a dinghy named Swallow. They meet the Blackett girls—Nancy and Peggy—who sail a dinghy named Amazon. Both families have a common foe in the Blackett's "Uncle Jim" Turner, whom they call Captain Flint.[14] Residing on his lake houseboat and there writing his memoirs, Captain Flint seems to have no time for the children. The children camp together on Wild Cat Island, where they play, have adventures, boat, and fish. Here is a fishing episode:

> So they rode ashore, and fastened a big stone to the other end of the anchor rope. Then they rode back to another place not far away. Roger let go the anchor, and Susan lowered the stone over the stern of the boat. This time Swallow rested broadside onto the wind, and did not swing at all. But they found it was

13. Grahame, *Wind in the Willows*, ch. 7, "The Piper at the Gates of Dawn." The book was heard on BARD.

14. In some ways, Uncle Jim represents Arthur Ransome, the author of the series.

no good fishing on the windward side, because the wind, even though there was so little of it, brought the floats in under the boat. So they all four fished on the same side. As the boat was not swinging, this did not matter, and everybody tried to watch all four floats at once.

"Who's float will go first?" said Roger.

"Mine," said Titty. "It's bobbing already."

"Look out, John," said Susan. "Your float isn't there."

John looked around. His float was gone. He pulled. The top of his rod bent and jerked, and up came a fat little perch with bright red fins and dark green bars on his sides. "That's one, anyhow," said John, as he put on another minnow.

After that the perch came fast, one after another. Sometimes three floats bobbed together. There was soon a pile of perch in the bottom of the boat.

Roger was counting them "Twelve, thirteen, fourteen. . . ."

"Where is your float, Roger?" said the mate.

"And look at your rod," said Titty.

Roger jumped up and caught hold of his jerking rod, which he had put down while he was counting the catch. He felt a fish at the end of his line. Just as he was bringing it to the top there was a great swirl in the water, and his rod suddenly pulled down again. Roger hung on as hard as he could, and his rod was bent almost into a circle.

"It's a shark! It's a shark!" he shouted.

Something huge was moving about in the water, deep down, pulling the rod this way and that.

"Let him have line off the reel," said John, but Roger held on.

Suddenly a mottled green fish, a yard long, with a dark black and white underneath, came to the top. It lifted an enormous head right out of the water, and opened a great white mouth, and shook itself. A little perch flew high into the air. Roger's rod straightened. For a moment the great fish lay close to the top of the water, looking wickedly at the crew of the Swallow as they looked at it. Then, with a twist of its tail that made a great twirling splash in the water, it was gone. Roger brought in the little perch. It was dead, and its sides were marked with deep gashes from the great teeth of the pike.

"I say," said Roger, "do you think it's really safe to bathe in this place?"[15]

15. Ransome, *Swallows and Amazons*, 79–81.

The pike got away, but the children continued to swim in the lake.

In other doings, the children discover a plot by burglars to steal Uncle Jim's memoirs. They manage to thwart the theft and save the manuscript. It all makes for an exciting and satisfying story.

In the 2016 film version of *Swallows and Amazons*, we see the children fishing and, later, cooking their catch—a trout, not perch—by mashing it up in a skillet! (By the way, in the film version, the burglars turn out to be Russian spies.)

Novelist Lane Walker's *The Fishing Chronicles* is also a children's book series. Offering five different adventures from river-raft camping and fishing to trying to win an ice-fishing contest for money to save the family's bait shop, the series offers compelling tales for those five to 11 years old.

Yet one more watery children's novel to consider is *The Borrowers Afloat*, a classic by Mary Norton. In it, the tiny people known as Borrowers, needing to find a new home in which to borrow things, wash down an old home's kitchen drain. They end up in a teapot, floating down a river at flood tide. No fish or fishing are involved in this particular adventure. Still, the tale is watery.[16]

To close out this children's chapter, let me include a story that clearly mentions trout fishing. Roald Dahl's *Danny, the Champion of the World* has a young English boy, Danny, and his dad, William, living in a Gypsy caravan. William runs a filling station and fixes cars for a living. Some evenings at dusk, he poaches pheasants in the woods of a rich, selfish, and unneighborly landowner, Mr. Hazell. Danny ultimately joins his much beloved father in this nighttime "work." The two are sometimes accompanied by the town's old doctor, a small but spritely man. On one occasion, Doc Spencer tells Danny how he also poaches trout. He asks the lad,

> "Do you know how to catch a trout, Danny, without using a rod and line?"
>
> "No," I said. "How?"
>
> "You tickle him."
>
> "Tickle him?"
>
> "Yes," the doctor said. "Trout, you see, like to lie close in to the river bank. So you go creeping along the bank until you see a big one . . . and you come up behind him . . . and you lie down on your tummy . . . and then slowly, very slowly, you lower your

16. Mary Norton's *The Borrowers* was heard on BARD.

> hand into the water behind him . . . and you slide it underneath him and you begin to stroke his belly up and down with the tip of one finger. . . ."
>
> "Will he really let you do that?" I asked.
>
> "He loves it!" the doctor said. "He loves it so much he sort of dozes off. And as soon as he dozes off you quickly grab hold of him and flip him out of the water and on to the bank."
>
> "That works!" my father said. But only a great artist can do it. I take my hat off to you, sir."[17]

As the book closes, Danny and his father go down the road to a stream to fish for rainbow trout—method of taking not revealed.

We now conclude this genre of fishing tales, well aware that children's stories and rhymes that involve fish, fishing, or water typically fire the imagination, sometimes teach a lesson, and always delight both youngsters and elders.

17. Dahl, *Danny*, 79–80.

Chapter 9

Poems

Poems of fishers, angling, and the deep are many. They span cultures and time, constituting another genre of tales.

In Chapters 1 and 4 of this book, we noted that *The Odyssey* by Homer has fishing references in Book 12. Those passages come to us in the poetic meter known as dactylic hexameter. Let me repeat one of the passages and, thereby, introduce the distinctive ninth genre of literature for fishing tales:

> A man surfcasting on a point of rock
> For bass and mackerel,
> Whipping his long rod
> To drop sinker and the bait far out,
> Will hook a fish
> And rip it from the surface
> To dangle, wriggling through the air.[1]

Another ancient writer who alludes to fly fishing is the Roman poet Ovid (43 B.C.E.–17 C.E.). As noted earlier, in *The Art of Love*, he suggests that "angling with a red cloth on a hook" as well as "sweet poetry" are two ways to catch one's quarry—fish or lover—by "attractive deception"!

Leaving antiquity behind, let's fast-forward to more recent centuries for other verses on angling. One of the best-known rhymes about fishing in the English language is some version of this:

> When the wind is from the East
> The fishing is the least.
> When the wind is from the West
> Fishing is the best.

1. Homer, *Odyssey* (Fitzgerald), bk 12, lines 300–305.

When the wind is from the South
It blows the bait in the fish's mouth.
[And, as I have always heard it . . .]
When the wind is from the North
Stay home!

Professor Henry Hughes of Western Oregon University has compiled an excellent collection of poems about fishing in *The Art of Angling: Poems About Fishing*.[2] The book contains over 120 poems in the public domain, including ones by Germany's Johann Wolfgang von Goethe; Scotland's Sir Walter Scott; England's Samuel Butler and William Cowper; America's Robert Service, Richard Brautigan, Mary Oliver, Margaret Atwood, and Benjamin Franklin. Several Japanese and Chinese poets are also included. The poet with the most poems in the collection is Isaac McLellan, an American fisher-poet, yet he was previously unknown to me. Eight of his poems appear in Hughes' collection. Below are two verses from "The Angler's Chant":

Ah, the shriek of the reel, the trout-fisher's reel!
    No sound is so sweet to the ear;
The hum of the line, the buzz of the wheel!
    Where the crystalline brook runs so clear.

Then fling the light tackle with delicate cast,
    Let your fly like a cobweb alight,
A dash and a splash, and the victim is fast,
    While your reel sings a song of delight.[3]

Another of McLellan's poems, "Reminiscences," is about fishing beneath the old ropewalk at the foot of Boston Common. The memory includes

Our slender, homely fish-rods then
Would line the friendly pier,
And oh, what gleeful shouts arose,
What gay, light-hearted cheer,
As each one jerk'd the shiny prize,
The ribb'd, the struggling prey,
That filled our wicker creels with wealth,
Our hearts with joy that day![4]

2. Hughes, *Art of Angling*. Another source of fly-fishing poems—all by contemporary poets, such as Dave Motes and David Salamone—is the website Fly Anglers Online Poet's Creek, https://www.flyanglersonline.com/lighterside/poetscreek/.

3. Hughes, *Art of Angling*, 34.

4. Hughes, *Art of Angling*, 80.

McLellan also wrote poems about sea bass, pompano, blackfish, and brook trout.

Hughes' collection also includes works from the early 18th-century nature-romantics John Gay, author of "Rural Sports, A Georgic," and James Thomson, who penned "The Seasons: Spring." Each of these poets have flowery verses on fishing. Gay, for example, rejecting all other means of fishing—such as spearing, netting, pond draining, worm- or insect-impaling—chooses fly fishing.

> Let me, less cruel, cast the feather'd hook,
> With pliant rod athwart the pebbled brook,
> Silent along the mazy margin stray,
> And with the fur-wrought fly delude the prey.[5]

Hughes includes my all-time best-loved poem involving fishing. It is William Butler Yeats' "The Song of Wandering Aengus." It begins:

> I went out to the hazel wood,
> Because a fire was in my head,
> And cut and peeled a hazel wand,
> And hooked a berry to a thread;
> And when white moths were on the wing,
> And moth-like stars were flickering out,
> I dropped the berry in a stream
> And caught a little silver trout.
>
> When I had laid it on the floor
> I went to blow the fire a flame,
> But something wrestled on the floor,
> And someone called me by my name:
> It had become a glimmer and girl
> With apple blossom in her hair
> Who called me by my name and ran
> And faded through the brightening air.
>
> Though I am old with wandering
> Through hollow lands and hilly lands,
> I will find out where she has gone,
> And kiss her lips and take her hands.
> And walk among long dappled grass,
> And pluck till time and times are done,
> The silver apples of the moon,
> The golden apples of the sun.[6]

5. Hughes, *Art of Angling*, 126.
6. Hughes, *Art of Angling*, 126.

Wandering Aengus Pursuing the Glimmering Girl

For his playwriting, Yeats longed for appreciation. Sadly, though, his stage offerings were dismissed by the Dublin elites and ignored by the general public. Such rejection had him longing for a countryman, a more appreciative reader, the fisherman.

> Although I can see him still,
> The freckled man who goes
> To a grey place on a hill
> In grey Connemara clothes
> At dawn to cast his flies. . . .
> Climbing up to a place
> Where stone is dark under froth,

And the down turn of his wrist
When the flies drop in the stream:
A man who does not exist,
A man who is but a dream;
And cried, "Before I am old
I shall have written him one
Poem maybe as cold
And passionate as the dawn."[7]

Another excellent poem in Hughes' collection is John Donne's "The Bait." Some may recognize the poem's first line as being identical to the first line of Christopher Marlowe's "The Passionate Shepherd to His Love" but may not realize that every verse in "The Bait" references fishing. Here is the first:

Come live with me, and be my love,
And we will some new pleasures prove
Of golden sands, and crystal brooks,
With silken lines, and silver hooks.[8]

The bard of all bards, of course, is William Shakespeare. I do not know if he ever actually fished, but, certainly, Shakespeare uses angling imagery in *Antony and Cleopatra*. In this play, Cleopatra and her handmaid Charmion talk about how she is going to catch Mark Antony, to wit:

Cleopatra
Give me mine angle; we'll to the river. There,
My music playing far off, I will betray
Tawny-finned fishes. My bended hook shall pierce
Their slimy jaws, and as I draw them up
I'll think them every one an Antony,
And say, "Aha! You're caught."

Charmion
'Twas merry when
You wagered on your angling when your diver
Did hang a salt fish on his hook, which he
With fervency drew up.

Cleopatra
That time–oh, times![9]

7. Hughes, *Art of Angling*, 57.
8. Hughes, *Art of Angling*, 118.
9. Hughes, *Art of Angling*, 41.

Fifty years after Shakespeare, Izaak Walton waxes eloquent on freshwater fishing in his poem "The Angler's Song," referenced previously in Chapter 4. He begins with a nod to friends engaged in various sports and ends with a declaration to follow in the way of Christ and Christ's fisher friends.

Who hunts, doth oft in danger ride;
Who hawks, lures oft both far and wide;
Who uses games, may often prove
A loser; but who falls in love
  Is fetter'd in fond Cupid's snare:
  My angle breeds me no such care.

Of recreation there is none
So free as fishing is alone;
All other pastimes do no less
Than mind and body both possess;
  My hand alone my work can do,
  So I can fish and study too.

I care not, I, to fish in seas—
Fresh rivers best my mind do please,
Whose sweet calm course I contemplate,

. . .
And when the timorous Trout I wait
To take, and he devours my bait.
How poor a thing, sometimes I find,
Will captivate a greedy mind;
  And when none bite, I praise the wise,
  Whom vain allurements ne'er surprise.

. . .
The first men that our Saviour dear
Did choose to wait upon Him here,
Bless'd fishers were, and fish the last
Food was that He on earth did taste:
  I therefore strive to follow those
  Whom He to follow Him hath chose.[10]

A century after Walton came John Bunyan, author of *The Pilgrim's Progress.* In that epic poem, Bunyan uses angling imagery to describe how difficult it is to catch souls.

10. Walton, *Compleat Angler*, 93–4. For other Walton poems, see Chapter 4, "Classic Literature," of this anthology.

You see the ways the Fisher-man doth take
To catch the fish; what engines doth he make?
Behold how he engageth all his wits.
Also his snares, lines, angles, hooks, and nets.
Yet fish there be, that neither hook, nor line,
They must be grop'd for, and be tickled too,
Or they will not be catch'd, whate'er you do.[11]

Such is a truth to which many a preacher and missionary will attest.

By the way, in his poem "Upon the Fish on the Water," Bunyan penned the line "water is the fish's element," which line, three centuries later, is repeated by Old Nick in David James Duncan's novel *The River Why*.[12]

Poet Jean de La Fontaine (1621–1695) has a couple of poems that tell interesting fish tales. "The Little Fish and the Fisherman" is a recasting into verse of what was prose in an Aesop fable.

A little Fish will larger grow, in time,
If God will only grant him life; and yet
To let him free out of the tangling net
Is folly; and I mean it, though I rhyme:
The catching him again is not so sure, c'est tout.
A little Carp, who half a summer knew,
Was taken by an angler's crafty hook.
"All count," the man said; "this begins my feast:
I'll put it in my basket." "Here, just look!"
Exclaimed, in his own way, the tiny beast.
"Now what on earth can you, sir, want with me?
I'm not quite half a mouthful, as you see.
Let me grow up, and catch me when I'm tall,
Then some rich epicure will buy me dear.
But now you'll want a hundred, that is plain,
Aye, and as much again,
To make a dish; and what dish after all?
Why good for nothing." "Good for nothing, eh?"
Replied the Angler. "Come, my little friend,
Into the pan you go; so end.
Your sermon pleases me, exceedingly.
To-night we'll try

11. Hughes, *Art of Angling*, 125.

12. See Chapter 6 of this book.

How you will fry.

[Then comes the moral:]

The present, not the future, tense
Is that preferred by men of sense?
The one is sure that you have got.
The other, verily, is not.[13]

The second angling-related Jean de La Fontaine poem is "The Fishes and the Shepherd Who Played the Flute." In it, a shepherd tries by reasoned argument and honeyed words, as well as by his charming songs, to entice the fish to come to his lady Annette's bait. The fish are not persuaded. The poem ends as follows:

O ye shepherds, whose sheep men are,
To trust in reason never dare.
The arts of eloquence sublime
Are not within your calling;
Your fish were caught, from oldest time,
By dint of nets and hauling.[14]

Another poem of water—in particular, ocean water—is Samuel Taylor Coleridge's "The Rime of the Ancient Mariner" with its lines from my dusty college textbook:

Water, water, everywhere,
And all the boards did shrink.
Water, water, everywhere,
Nor any drop to drink.[15]

Coleridge's poem, written in 1798, is lengthy, but, once upon a time, most American high-school students pondered it in English Lit.

A "fishier" poem, not as likely to appear in high-school textbooks, is Alfred Lord Tennyson's "The Miller's Daughter," which suggests that fishing detracts man from romantic thoughts.

I met in all the close green ways,
    While walking with my line and rod,
The wealthy miller's mealy face,
    Like the moon in an ivy-tod.
He looked so jolly and so good—
    While fishing in the milldam-water,

13. La Fontaine, "Little Fish and the Fisherman."

14. La Fontaine, "Fishes and the Shepherd."

15. Coleridge, "Rime of the Ancient Mariner," 433.

I laughed to see him as he stood,
  And dreamt not of the miller's daughter.[16]

One angling story-poem from the 19th century is Henry Wadsworth Longfellow's "The Angler's Song." Here are two of the verses:

Where the embracing ivy holds
Close the hoar elm in its folds,
In the meadow's fenny land,
And the winding river sweeps
Through its shallows and still deeps,
Silent with my rod I stand.

But when sultry suns are high
Underneath the oak I lie
As it shades the water's edge,
And I mark my line, away
In the wheeling eddy, play,
Tangling with the river's edge.[17]

A poem written in 1877 but not published for another 30 years is Gerard Manley Hopkins' trout-imaging poem of praise, "Pied Beauty":

Glory be to God for dappled things—
  For skies of couple-colour as a brinded cow;
  For rose-moles all in stipple upon trout that swim;
Fresh-firecoal chestnut-falls; finches' wings.
  Landscape plotted and pieced—fold, fallow, and plough;
  And all trades, their gear and tackle and trim.
All things counter, original, spare, strange;
  Whatever is fickle, freckled (who knows how?)
  With swift, slow; sweet, sour; adazzle, dim;
He fathers-forth whose beauty is past change:
  Praise him.[18]

The German brown trout with its haloed black and red spots on a brassy brown body surely falls under the description of "pied" and "dappled."

Another poem recognizing fish and a fish's water is "The Perch" by Seamus Heaney, Irish poet and recipient of the Nobel Prize in Literature. His poem glorifies perch in their natural setting of clear water and clay banks where the alder beds afford their concealment. [19]

16. Hughes, *Art of Angling*, 54.
17. Longfellow, "Angler's Song."
18. Hopkins, "Pied Beauty."
19. Heaney, *Electric Light*, 4.

A contemporary of Yeats was Rupert Brooke, killed in World War I. Before dying, he wrote a poem called "Heaven," envisioning human eternity from the world of fish.

> Fish say, they have their Stream and Pond;
> But is there anything Beyond?
> This life cannot be All, they swear,
> For how unpleasant if it were!
> One may not doubt that, somehow, Good
> Shall come of Water and of Mud;
> And, sure, the reverent eye must see
> A Purpose in Liquidity.[20]

A verse from "Eternal Father, Strong To Save," sometimes referred to as "The Navy Hymn," aligns with Brooke's trust and faith:

> Eternal Father, strong to save,
> Whose arm hath bound the restless wave,
> Who bidd'st the mighty ocean deep
> Its own appointed limits keep;
> Oh, hear us when we cry to Thee,
> For those in peril on the sea![21]

Moving from the sacred to the profane, a simple doggerel poem on fishing must be inserted: Edgar Guest's "A Boy and His Dad." Offered early in the last century, it was quite popular then. Here are the first and last verses:

> A boy and his dad on a fishing-trip—
> There is a glorious fellowship!
> Father and son and the open sky
> And the white clouds lazily drifting by,
> And the laughing stream as it runs along
> With the clicking reel like a martial song,
> And the father teaching the youngster gay
> How to land a fish in the sportsman's way.
> . . .
> A boy and his dad on a fishing-trip—
> Builders of life's companionship!

20. Brooke, "Heaven."

21. "Eternal Father, Strong To Save" was written by the Reverend William Whiting (1825–1878) and is still found in military and church hymnals.

Oh, I envy them, as I see them there
Under the sky in the open air,
For out of the old, old long-ago
Come the summer days that I used to know,
When I learned life's truths from my father's lips
As I shared the joy of his fishing-trips.[22]

Genio C. Scott has written a book called *Fishing in American Waters.* Poems are sprinkled throughout the pages with a special section on the poetry of angling, including Jesse E. Dow's poem "Autumn":

The patient angler threads the winding brook,
Tempting the dainty trout with gilded bait;
And ever and anon, as fleecy clouds
Pass o'er the sun, the fish voracious darts
From the cool shadows of some mossy bank,
Swallows the bait with one convulsive act,
And learns too late that death was at the feast;
While the glad sportsman feels the sudden jerk,
And plays his victim with extended line,
Swiftly he darts, and through the glittering rings
The silken line is drawn with ringing sound,
Till, wearied out with struggling that but serves
To drive the barbed weapon deeper still,
He seeks his quiet shelter 'neath the bank,
And thence in triumph to the shore is borne,
A prize that well rewards a day of toil.[23]

Also in Scott's collection is a cautionary tale about poaching fish by English poet and humorist Thomas Hood.

Bill Blossom was a nice young man,
And drove the Bury coach;
But bad companions were his bane,
And egg'd him on to poach.

. . .

But going to his usual Hants,
Old Cheshire [the sheriff] laid his plots:
He got entrapp'd by legal Berks,
And lost his life in Notts.[24]

22. Guest, "Boy and His Dad."
23. Scott, *Fishing in American Waters,* 141.
24. Scott, *Fishing in American Waters,* 152.

Notts, assuredly, is a county jail.

Contemporary angling poems may be found that relate to fly fishing. The first, penned by Ron Rash, is titled "Speckled Trout":

> Water-flesh gleamed like mica:
> orange fins, red flankspots, a char
> shy as ginseng, found only
> in spring-flow gaps, the thin clear
> of faraway creeks no map
> could name. My cousin showed me
> those hidden places. I loved
> how we found them, the way we
> followed no trail, just stream-sound
> tangled in rhododendron,
> to where slow water opened
> a hole to slip a line in,
> and lift as from a well bright
> shadows of another world,
> held in my hand, their color
> already starting to fade.[25]

The second, by Michael Sowder, is called "Fishing, His Birthday" and is rich with names of flies.

> With adams, caddis, tricos, light cahills,
> blue-wing olives, royal coachmen, chartreuse trudes,
> green drakes, blue duns, black gnats, Nancy quills,
> Joe's hoppers, yellow humpies, purple chutes,
> prince nymphs, pheasant tails, Eileen's hare's ears,
> telicos, flashbacks, Jennifer's muddlers,
> Frank bugs, sow bugs, zug bugs, autumn splendors,
> woolly worms, black buggers, Kay's gold zuddlers,
> clippers, tippet, floatant, spools of leader,
> tin shot, lead shot, hemostats, needle nose,
> rod, reel, vest, net, boots, cap, shades and waders,
> gortex shell and one bent marabou—
> I wade in a swirl of May-colored water,
> cast a fine gray quill, the last tie of my father.[26]

A poem from the end of the 20th century is Ted Kooser's "Casting Reels," which strongly suggests deeper stories of working stiffs, beginning with their fishing gear:

25. Rash, "Speckled Trout."

26. Sowder, "Fishing, His Birthday."

You find them at flea markets
and yard sales, old South Bends
and Pfluegers, with fancy engraving,
knurled knobs and pearl handles,
spooled with fraying line
of long stories into
silence, not just exaggerated tales
of walleyes, bass, and catfish,
but of hardworking men
who on Saturdays sought out
the solace of lakes, who on weekdays
at desks, or standing on ladders,
or next to clattering machines
played out their youth and strength
waiting to set the hook, and then,
in their sixties, felt the line go slack
and reeled the years back empty.
They are the ones who got away.[27]

Another "line going slack" consideration is "The Fisherman's Prayer." My fly-fishing compadres Bob Tucker (1931–2020) and Stan Harwood (1937–2021) always carried a copy of it in their wallet.

God grant that I may live
To fish until my dying day
And when it comes to my last cast
I then most humbly pray
When in the Lord's safe landing net
I'm peacefully asleep
That in His mercy I'll be judged
Good enough to keep.

27. White, *Round Boys Great Adventures*, 150.

CHAPTER 10

Gone Fishin' Songs

POEMS, WITH THEIR METER and rhyme, often are set to music, in which case they become "lyrics." Those lyrics typically tell a story or, at least, suggest one.

The song that inspired the title of this chapter is "Gone Fishin'." The song was made popular in 1951 when sung by Bing Crosby and Louis Armstrong. The song's most memorable lines speak about going fishing "instead of just a-wishin'." It is a delightful story of getting away from the work of hoeing for contented angling beside a "shady-wady pool." After considerable back-and-forth banter, Bing says to Louis that he, too, is hanging a "Gone Fishin'" sign on his door.[1]

The very best fish-story song that I've ever heard echoes the Selkie legends presented in Chapter 1. Here's the 1866 version of the song, popularized by Burl Ives in the 1950s:

> One night when I was lighting the glim,
> A'whistling a verse of the evening hymn,
> I saw by the light of the signal lamp,
> Mother looking awfully cold and damp;
> When a voice from the starboard cries out, "Ship, ahoy!"
> And there she was, floating on a buoy.
>
> . . .
>
> So I says, "Hello, Mother, how do you do,
> And how goes on my sisters two?"
> And she says, "You artful dar,
> You not got no sisters, nor yet no pa;
> Your pa was wrecked with several pals,
> And digested by the canni-bals.

1. Charles and Nick Kenny, "Gone Fishin'," 1950, in Bethge, "The Best Fishing Songs of All Time." Since copyright laws regarding lyrics are strict, *prosaic* paraphrase must sometimes replace *poetic* fullness. I encourage the reader to look up the complete song lyrics for every song mentioned.

And your sisters—one was cooked in a dish
And the other one is the talking fish.[2]

Burl Ives ends the song by explaining that the mermaid mother swims off, exclaiming, "To hell with the keeper of the Eddystone Light," the father of her children.

Angry Mermaid to the Keeper of the Eddystone Light

A well-known song from the 19th-century Southern tradition, made popular in the 20th by folk singer Woody Guthrie, among other performers, is "The Crawdad Song":

You get a line, I'll get a pole, honey.
You get a line, I'll get a pole, babe.
You get a line, I'll get a pole,
We'll go down to the crawdad hole.

2. London, "Man at the Nore." For the Burl Ives version called "The Eddystone Light," see the bibliography.

Honey, babe of mine.[3]

Guthrie is also noted for his "Talking Fishing Blues," so full of fun angling tales.

I went down to the fishing hole,
And I set down with my fishing pole;
Somethin' grabb'd my hook and it got my bait
And jerked me out in the middle of the lake.
Huh it was some jump boy,
I got sunk, kinda baptized on credit.

Fishin' down on th' muddy bank,
Felt a pull an' give a big yank,
I drug out three old rubber boots,
A Ford radiator an' a Chevrolet coop
(Nothin' but Junk, so I handed it in
For National Defence).

. . .

Jumped in the river and went down deep,
There was a hundred pound cat-fish lying there asleep,
Well I jumped on his back and rode him all aroun'
Saddled him up and I came into town.
People came runnin', lookin', dogs a-barkin'
(Kids a-squallin').

Early one mornin' I took me a notion,
To go out fishin' in the middle of the ocean,
Well, throwed me a line, I got me a shark,
I didn't get him home till way past dark.
(Was he a man-eater, tough customer.
But he wasn't quite tough enough.)[4]

Woody Guthrie's protégé Bob Dylan, recipient of the 2016 Nobel Prize in Literature, has written a watery ballad with dialogue verses between two lovers. In the first verse, the woman says that she'll be sailing away across the ocean and asks whether there is something that she can send her lover once she lands. He rejects her offer. Undaunted, she asks again, but the answer again is no; only her return will do. The two lovers go back and forth, him stating that diamonds from the deepest ocean could not substitute for her absence. Finally, the lover at home hears from his traveling sweetheart that

3. Guthrie, "Crawdad Song." This folk song evolved from Anglo-American traditions and African-American blues.

4. Guthrie, "Talking Fishing Blues."

she may not be returning to him. The rejected lover accepts his fate, wishes her well, and asks, at last, for her to send him "boots of Spanish leather" (the title of the song).[5]

The long-running 1960s television sitcom *The Andy Griffith Show* used as its theme music the song "The Fishin' Hole," which includes these lines:

Well now, take down your fishing pole
And meet me at the fishing hole
We may not get a bite all day
But don't you rush away
What a great place to rest your bones
And mighty fine for skipping stones
You'll feel fresh as a lemonade
A-setting in the shade.[6]

A full versing of the brief introductory song—often whistled—would include these lines:

They'll be you, me, and old dog Trey
To do the time away
If we don't hook a perch or bass
We'll cool our toes in dewy grass.[7]

Blues musician Taj Mahal, the Nitty Gritty Dirt Band, Henry Thomas, and many others have recorded their own versions of an angling song called "Fishin' Blues." Here is a representative verse of this song, originally penned by Chris Smith:

I bet your life your lovin' wife
Can catch more fish than you.
Any fish bite if you've got good bait.
Here's a little somethin' I would like to relate.
Any fish bite, you've got good bait.
I'm a-goin' a-fishin', yes, I'm a-goin a-fishin',
I'm a-goin' a-fishin' too.[8]

As with the previous fishing songs shared in this chapter, this one is melodic, rhythmic, and fun.

5. Dylan, "Boots of Spanish Leather."
6. Sloane, "Fishin' Hole."
7. Sloane, "Fishin' Hole."
8. Smith, "Fishin' Blues."

Now let us move from popular secular music to sacred songs. A sampling of traditional Christian hymns that have water themes include

"Shall We Gather at the River?"

"Roll, Jordan, Roll"

"Crossing the Bar"

"Deep River"

"Down to the River to Pray"

We also have the Christmas carol "I Saw Three Ships Come Sailing In."

"Los peces en el río" ("The Fish in the River") is a traditional, though admittedly odd, paean in Spanish to the Virgin Mary, who bore the Christ child. Here is one verse translated into English:

> But look how the fish drink in the river,
> But look how they drink to see God being born,
> They drink, they drink, and then they drink again,
> The fish in the river to see God being born.[9]

As noted in Chapter 3, the early Christian church used F.I.S.H.—IXTHMUS in Greek—as an acronym for "Jesus Christ, God's Son and Savior." Some biblical accounts of Jesus and fish have made their way into songs. A Sunday-school song called "Five Loaves and Two Fishes" tells of a boy who heard Jesus speaking to a hungry crowd by the seashore and decided to share his lunch of bread and fish. On Christian radio, one may hear a song about the "miraculous draught of fish" that Jesus enabled his fellow fishers to net in the Sea of Galilee. It was after that great catch that Jesus called these particular followers to become "fishers of men." The words, originally in Spanish, of this hymn reflect the fishers' new calling:

> You have come down to the lakeshore
> Seeking neither the wise nor the wealthy,
> But only asking for me to follow.
>   O Jesus, you have looked into my eyes,
>   Kindly smiling, you have called out my name.
>   On the sand I have abandoned my small boat;
>   Now with you I will seek other seas.
> You who have fished other waters;
> You, the longing of souls that are yearning:

9. *"Los peces en el río."*

As loving Friend, you have come to call me.
. . . I will seek other seas.[10]

In addition to hearing folk music in coffeehouses and hymns in church sanctuaries, one also might listen on seaport docks for musical material with fishy or watery references. Especially rich are sea shanties. One such song is "A Whale of a Tale" written by Al Hoffman and Norman Gimbel and sung by actor Kirk Douglas in the 1954 movie *20,000 Leagues Under the Sea*. One verse talks about flapping fish as well as girls the sailor knew. The last verse is about Mimi the Mermaid, who would kiss the lucky sailor at his request. His luck, unfortunately, ran out when Mimi the Mermaid swapped him for a trout. Imagine the indignity![11]

Other sea shanties to consider are "Blow the Man Down," "What Shall We Do With a Drunken Sailor?" and "Blood Red Roses." Even more shanties can be found in the movie *Fisherman's Friends*, including "Fisherman's Blues" in which the songster wishes that he were a fisherman casting his line with "abandonment and love" under the sky.[12]

Another sea-related story in a song is Godfrey Marks' 1880 "Sailing, Sailing" with the chorus

Sailing, sailing,
Over the bounding main,
For many a stormy wind shall blow
Ere Jack comes home again.[13]

Jack could be an impressed sailor on a British frigate sailing the Indian Ocean or, we could believe, a Minnesota fisher in a wee smack, trolling for salmon on Lake Superior. I like the latter idea, knowing that steelhead are there, too, making their winter run up the Canadian and U.S. rivers plied by hardcore fly fishers.

10. Gabárain, *"Tu has venido a la orilla."* A similarly themed hymn is "You Walk Along Our Shoreline."

11. Hoffman and Gimbel, "Whale of a Tale."

12. Scott and Wickham, "Fisherman's Blues."

13. Marks, "Sailing, Sailing."

Another place to look for songs about fishing, fish, or water is in stage musicals. *The Pirates of Penzance* and *South Pacific* suggest possibilities. However, if angling songs are what we seek, more promising are the opera *Porgy and Bess* and the musical *Carousel.*

Besides the namesake characters in *Porgy and Bess* are Clara and Jake. The couple has a child to whom Clara sings about summertime when the living is easy and the fish are jumpin'. The "fish are jumpin'" line alludes to the fact that life on Catfish Row near the docks in Charleston, South Carolina, is a fishing life, and Jake is a fisherman. One ominously dark day, he heads out to work the Blackfish Banks. A violent storm sweeps in, capsizing his boat, and Jake drowns. Living is no longer easy for Clara.[14]

One gets much closer to fish and a fishing story in the musical *Carousel.* The main characters are barker Billy Bigelow and millworker Julie Jordan. Secondary characters are Carrie Pipperidge and her fisherman beau, Enoch Snow. Carrie's delightful song "Mister Snow" reminds us of a truth seldom forgotten by those closest to those who angle. Carrie explains that her man returns every night in his round-bottomed boat with a net full of herring. At the beginning of their relationship, the fishy smell of him nearly knocked her over. But, once in love with Mr. Snow, the fragrance of fish on her man is her "fav'rite perfume."[15]

14. Heyward and Gershwin, "Summertime."

15. Hammerstein, "Mister Snow."

Three Songsters—Sailor, Fisher, and Cowboy

Moving away from Broadway, consider yet another venue for fishing and water songs, namely, places where country-and-western music is enjoyed—Nashville's Grand Ole Opry for example. Among the tunes played on stage there was "Long Gone Lonesome Blues" by Hank Williams, the hillbilly Shakespeare. This mournful tale, told in the first person, tells that the lovesick and lonesome singer went to a river to watch the fish swim, but, when he got there, his bad luck continued, for, jumping in, he found that the river was dry. The last verse relates that he plans to find an icy river in which he can jump and, thus, end his life and be "long gone."[16]

Other C&W songs have a stronger fish theme. One is "Fish and Whistle" by John Prine. A second is "Catch All the Fish" by Brad Paisley, a humorous song that includes three critical ingredients of many a modern fishing trip—fish, beer, and gasoline—with the emphasis on the first two. A third is simply called "Fishin'" and is by Elvin Bishop. My fishing friend Greg Walters cranks up this one every time that we head to the river. Its refrain repeats and repeats, "I'm goin' fish-fish, fish-fish, fish-fish, fishin'."[17]

16. Williams, "Long Gone Lonesome Blues."

17. Bishop, "Fishin'."

A fourth C&W offering about fishing is Otis Gibbs' talking-blues song called "Big Whiskers." It's about a giant river mudcat whom the singer says his grandfather hooked and lost when a youth. His grandpa then resolved never to cut his beard until he caught the fish for good. In advanced old age, with a beard that had grown down to the floor, Grandpa finally caught Big Whiskers. However, instead of keeping the fish, the old man respected the old fish by first removing all the lures and rusty hooks stuck in the fish's crooked mouth and then letting him go. Grandpa, in turn, cleaned up his own look by whacking off his big whiskers.[18]

Songwriter-vocalist Dar Williams has a song named "Fishing in the Morning." It resonates familiarly with anglers when it talks about a before-dawn ride, fishing rods knocking together in the back seat, the truck running well, and "everything fine."[19]

Outdoors writer Ed Godfrey of *The Oklahoman* newspaper ranks "The Five Pound Bass" by Robert Earl Keen as the best fishing song ever.[20] Keen's ballad tells a complete fishing story.

> Up this morning before the sun
> Fixed me some coffee and a honey bun
> Jumped in my pickup and gave her the gas
> I'm goin' out to catch a five pound bass
>
> Jumped in my jon-boat, I stow my gear
> I fire her up and when I am in the clear
> I sail across that water as smooth as glass
> Ready, here I come, you five pound bass
>
> I find the perfect spot, some old dead trees
> Back in a canyon where you can't feel no breeze
> I tie my lure, I make my cast
> It's breakfast time, you five pound bass
>
> That old sun is rising, that water is clear
> I watch my lure as it's flying through the air
> I see a ripple, I hear a splash
> Lord have mercy, it's a five pound bass
>
> [Spoken:] That's a five pound bass, son
> Aw it's big as a god damned baby.[21]

18. Gibbs, "Big Whiskers—Otis Gibbs (Official Video)." See the children's book *Jangles* for a similar telling. *Jangles* is referenced in Chapter 8 of this anthology.

19. Williams, "Fishing in the Morning."

20. Godfrey, "Best Fishing Songs."

21. Keen, "Five Pound Bass."

Let me nominate the Eagles' song "Take It to the Limit," [22] as the best trout-fishers' song. Like several songs above, it is not an angling, fish, or water story per se, but, for this angler, it is strongly associated with many excellent fishing trips. Whenever my fishing compadre of 60 years, Bruce Kuster, and I approach Fort Smith, Montana, on the Bighorn River, we roll down the car windows, dial in the song, crank up the speakers, and sing at the top of our lungs about highways and signs and limits we need not count, since catch-and-release is our practice. Our alternative interpretation of "limit" in this song means taking life to the top of the fly-fisher's world—which the Bighorn River comes as close as any to being.

In concluding this chapter, mention must be made of classical music wherein there also are fishing, fish, and water stories, wordless but moving. Imagine listening to George Frederic Handel's *Water Music* on the Thames tributaries fished by Izaak Walton. Or consider Franz Schubert's *Trout Quintet*. Listening to it, one can well imagine German browns moving in the watery currents. Another orchestral offering is Bedřich Smetana's *Vltava*, a symphonic poem about the fabled river winding through the Czech Republic, one in which this fisher had a "Bohemian grand slam," catching brown trout, rainbows, grayling, chub, and roach.

22. Meisner et al., "Take It to the Limit."

Chapter 11

Fishing Humor

When one hears mention of a fishing story, one expects the truth to be stretched, outright lies to be told, and at least one whopper. The following riddle expresses this notion.

Question
What is the only thing known to grow after it is dead?
Answer
A fish.

Fishers laugh at themselves in books, in magazine articles, in boats, along shores, and around campfires, and, then, there are the cartoons tacked on bulletin boards in bait shops. Humorous jokes and writing constitute a distinct genre in the angling corpus.

Let us begin with books of fishing humor. First and foremost among the fishing humorists is Patrick F. McManus. His delightful book titles themselves often inspire a smile or a chuckle:

A Fine and Pleasant Misery (1978)

They Shoot Canoes, Don't They? (1981)

Never Sniff a Gift Fish (1983)

The Grasshopper Trap (1985)

Rubber Legs and White Tail-Hairs (1987)

The Night the Bear Ate Goombaw (1989)

Real Ponies Don't Go Oink! (1991)

The Good Samaritan Strikes Again (1992)

How I Got This Way (1994)

Never Cry "Arp!" and Other Great Adventures (1996)

Into the Twilight, Endlessly Grousing (1997)

The Deer on a Bicycle (2000)

The Bear in the Attic (2002)

Kerplunk! (2007)

The Horse in My Garage and Other Stories (2012)

Parts of these books have appeared in *Field and Stream* and *Outdoor Life* magazines. McManus wrote humorous essays and columns for these publications as well as others. Here are two passages from his columns:

> "There was one angler who believed that if you can't do a thing right, you shouldn't do it at all. A strict adherent to this philosophy, he hadn't been fishing once in the past 37 years."[1]
>
> "I have practiced ignorance most of my life and am intimately familiar with all its variations and applications. . . . Let us now apply ignorance to fly-fishing. Suppose your fly-fishing is like mine—no offense intended—and your main objective is somehow to get a fly to plop on the water in the hope that nearby there's a fish lacking in matters of style and taste."[2]

The characters in McManus' books are quirky, to say the least. When he writes about his childhood, the characters include his grandma, his gullible ma, his sister Troll, and especially Rancid Crabtree, his ever-unwashed mentor with whom he bumbles into outdoor adventures. When he speaks about his adult life, the characters are his wife, Bun; his often hoodwinked neighbor, Finley; and his hunting-and-fishing co-conspirator, Retch Sweeney. Whether in childhood or adult life, ever with him is his dog Strange.

They Shoot Canoes, Don't They? contains two stories well-illustrating McManus' zany sense of humor and imagination. He recounts that Rancid Crabtree and he were always trying to avoid anything taking effort or resembling work. So, one winter, to avoid pulling their ice-fishing shack onto the lake, they put a tall timber through the roof of the shack and affixed a canvas sail to it. Thus, they could sail out on the ice relatively easily. Ropes and pulleys operated it. Unfortunately, Rancid took the ropes inside the

1. Patrick McManus, "I'll Get to It—Someday," in Krebs, "17 Hilarious Pat McManus Quotes."

2. Patrick McManus, "I'll Get to It—Someday," in Krebs, "17 Hilarious Pat McManus Quotes."

shack just as McManus dropped the pin in the shack's outside door latch. Suddenly, the wind whipped up to blow their makeshift craft a mile down the lake. Rancid's walk back was long, hard, and, of course, against the wind. "So much for labor-saving ingenuity," McManus concludes.[3]

Ice-Fishing Shack Blowing Down the Lake

My favorite McManus tale is "The Sensuous Angler," which appears in *They Shoot Canoes*. In it, the author and Jennifer, a woman in Patrick's office, discover they both love to fish. So, they decide to spend an evening together, curing steelhead eggs with red dye. The dye gets on Patrick's shirt collar and looks like lipstick to his suspicious wife, Bun. Regardless, Patrick and Jennifer agree to do an evening of fileting fish together at her apartment, but it must occur, she says, when her husband, Hammer, who hates her doing anything fishy, is away. On the arranged evening, Jennifer greets Patrick at her apartment door in a spaghetti-strap negligee but immediately

3. McManus, *They Shoot Canoes*, 25–34.

excuses herself, saying she needs to " slip into something more comfortable"—patched baggy pants and a flannel shirt, fish scales still on it. McManus gives her a package of fresh-caught perch. This gift appeals to her much more than Hammer's gifts of red roses and dark chocolates. Jennifer and Patrick happily filet perch until Hammer, who works for The Godfather, unexpectedly returns. Jennifer quickly throws the fish in the freezer, then herself into Patrick's arms, saying, "Kiss me quick, so he won't suspect what we've been up to." Unperturbed about the kissing, Hammer smells the fish and flies into a rage. McManus, to escape, jumps out the kitchen window—the kitchen being on the *second* floor! He would have sprinted away, he says, "except it's so darn hard to sprint to safety when your legs are protruding from your armpits."[4]

I would be remiss not to mention another regular contributor to *Field and Stream*'s outdoor humor offerings, namely, Ed Zern. Some of his amusing magazine contributions were included in his books *A Fine Kettle of Fish Stories* and *How To Catch a Fisherman.*

The humorous fishing stories of Minnesotan Garrison Keillor were sometimes told on his weekly radio show, *A Prairie Home Companion.* Some stories were later available as recordings and in books. "Rex the Fishing Dog" is a great example. As Keillor tells it, Rex, not much more than a pup, once caught a fish in the shallows of Lake Wobegon and then, for years and years, patrolled the shores, hoping to repeat his achievement, but he never did. One evening, though, at a formal dinner party, Rex spotted a whole baked fish on the table. He jumped up, snatched it off the platter, and ran off. In doing so, the dog pulled off the tablecloth and most of the dishes.

In his "Guys on Ice" story, Keillor's uncle tells his nephew a mildly risqué version of how to ice fish: "You take a can of peas and spread it around the augured hole. So when a fish comes up to take a pea, you grab him!" Moreover, when the fishermen leave the shack to relieve themselves, Keillor says, "It is a comfort to a 14-year-old boy to know that, in the cold, *all men are created equal.*"[5]

Dave Barry, the well-known humorist who wrote a nationally syndicated column for the *Miami Herald*, tells a delightful story of fly fishing in Idaho. About the state, he says, "Many people think Idaho is nothing but potato farms, but nothing could be further from the truth: There are also beet farms." About fishing, he says:

4. McManus, *They Shoot Canoes*, 100–109.

5. These two stories probably exist in one of Keillor's many books. I retell them from memory of a Saturday-night broadcast and, later, from listening to an audio tape, such as *Lake Wobegon, Winter.*

> To catch trout, you have to engage in "fly casting," a kind of fishing that is very challenging, and here I am using "challenging" in the sense of "idiotic." . . . [W]ith "fly casting," you wade into the river and attempt to place a "fly"—a furry little hook thingy weighing slightly less than a hydrogen atom—on top of the water right where the trout are blooping. You do this by waving your fishing rod back and forth, using the following rhythm, as explained to us (I am not making this up) by [our guide] Susanne: "CO-ca CO-la, CO-ca CO-la." On your third CO-la, you point your arm forward, and the "fly," in a perfect imitation of nature, lands on your head. Or sometimes it forms itself into a snarl that cannot be untangled without the aid of a chainsaw AND a flamethrower.[6]

Known well in Colorado—and to me personally because we've fished together—is Rich Tosches, contributor to *Sports Illustrated*, the *Los Angeles Times*, and *The Denver Post* among other publications. His book *Zipping My Fly: Moments in the Life of an American Sportsman* includes a tale called "Pontoon Boat Envy: Where the Lunkers Lurk," which starts like this:

> Wading in the creeks and streams and rivers and wading into our lakes and ponds and reservoirs, however, apparently is not enough for the avid fly angler. Many years ago, according to fly-fishing historians, a man, probably named Chuck, stood on the shore of a lake, gazed out at the water, and spoke these prophetic words:
>
> "Someday we'll find a way to be out there, away
> from the shore, our gigantic asses submerged as we
> float around in some kind of tube."
> And the float tube was born.[7]

Tosches then tells about the development of the pontoon boat by the Dave Scadden Company with a particular concern:

> As you know, for centuries all personal fly-fishing pontoon craft have been either eleven feet long or twelve feet long. The guys with the smaller ones would invariably suffer from what psychiatrists call "pontoon boat envy." The guys with the twelve-footers would walk around with a big arrogant smile on their faces—right up until word got around the bar that they were having trouble "inflating the pontoon," if you know what I mean.[8]

6. Lyons, *Gigantic Book*, 434.
7. Tosches, *Zipping My Fly*, 125–26.
8. Tosches, *Zipping My Fly*, 127.

So, Tosches stayed with the belly boat, which had its own problems, to wit:

> The float-tube experience begins near the shoreline. Step number one involves pulling on your waders. If you forget this crucial step, you will find yourself sitting in a lake while wearing pants. After the waders are on, you put swim fins on your feet. If used correctly, these will propel you quickly across the water at speeds reaching one-one-hundredth of a mile per hour. As a bonus, they also put an unbelievable amount of stress on the ligaments and tendons in your knees, eventually crippling you and thus keeping you from skiing, which is a really stupid sport.
>
> After you've put on your waders and rubber swim fins, you climb into the tube and begin the graceful walk toward the water. There are two popular methods for doing this. The first is to walk forward. This allows the tips of your gigantic swim fins to catch the ground, toppling you face first into the lake. The more preferred method, of course, is to walk backward. Using this approach, the modern angler is able to stumble over something he cannot see and topple into the lake with the back of his head leading the way.[9]

Another float-tube complication is the wind. Tosches' friend and fellow outdoor writer Karl Licis took him fishing on Spinney Mountain Reservoir. Arriving at the lake, Licis warned, "The lake can get a little breezy at times." Still, they ventured forth with these results:

> I caught a nice rainbow, Karl hooked and landed a huge pike, and then the wind came.
>
> The wind came over the mountains and, to borrow a phrase made popular by Kansas trailer-home owners being interviewed on TV after watching their house take off, "sounded like a freight train."
>
> Suddenly I found myself in a tire tube that was riding up the front of four-foot waves and down the other side, into troughs so deep I expected to find Rush Limbaugh feeding in one of them. The wind was howling at 40 and 50 mph, I would learn from the National Weather Service the next day—after I was done choking Karl.
>
> And it was blowing parallel to the shore. No matter how hard I kicked the swim fins, I could not close the gap between myself and land. I was screaming and flailing my arms and kicking as hard as I could as I went past the spot on the shore where he was standing, having apparently anticipated the "little breeze."

9. Tosches, *Zipping My Fly,* 128–29.

> As I went sailing past frantically waving my hand at him, Karl responded by waving back.
>
> I washed up on a point that extended well out into the lake, some one and a half miles from where I was when the typhoon hit. When I crawled out of the float tube, I tried to stand up and went lurching sideways for about thirty feet, my knees aching and my thigh muscles burning and unable to hold my weight. I lay on my side on the gravel for about fifteen minutes thinking about what a wonderful experience this float-tube thing had been.
>
> And wondering if Karl's proctologist would return my landing net.[10]

In my personal library are other humor books, such as two by Milford Poltroon, *How To Fish Good* and *The Worst of the Wretched Mess News*, complete with original cartoon drawings and old-time photographs. I highly recommend both of these.

An unequivocally humorous novella is Richard Brautigan's *Trout Fishing in America*. This is a Jack Kerouac *On the Road*-type story, comical and satirical. The phrase "Trout Fishing in America" is used in many ways, as a *title*, a *character* in the story, a *modifier* for that character, a *hotel*, and the *act of fishing* itself. Brautigan uses the theme of trout fishing as a point of departure for thinly veiled and often comical critiques of mainstream American society and culture. Several symbolic objects reappear throughout the book, such as a mayonnaise jar, a Ben Franklin statue in San Francisco's Washington Square, and trout. They come into consideration in this abstract—all but incomprehensible—book, particularly when Brautigan, his wife, and their baby go on an extended fly-fishing trip through the Pacific Northwest.[11]

Let us now pick up one more humorous volume, fishily laced.

In 1956, the English—very English—author Rose Macaulay published *The Towers of Trebizond*. Ostensibly, the (somewhat autobiographical) novel is a travelogue of a journey through the Middle East told by a young woman named Laurie. Laurie goes on this trip with her adventurous Aunt Dot (a would-be missionary), Father Pigg (an Anglican priest), *and* a white camel. They travel to the ancient Byzantine city of Trebizond on the Black Sea. Once there, they make their way into Armenia toward Mount Ararat, where Noah's ark, according to tradition, first touched ground. En route, the group camps by a mountain stream from which they catch trout. All in the party seem to be fly-fishers, quite proper for English folk.

Laurie says about her family's religion:

10. Tosches, *Zipping My Fly*, 130.

11. Brautigan, *Trout Fishing in America*, see especially 37–42. Book heard on BARD.

> [We have] inherited a firm and tenacious adherence to the Church of our country. With it has come down to most of us a great enthusiasm for catching fish . . . .
>
> Our family have been much given to this pursuit. Inheriting the fishponds of the Sussex abbey which they so warily angled for and hooked in 1539, they took for their crest three pikes couchant, with the motto "Semper pesco," (it was as masters of trawling-fleets that they had acquired their wealth in the fifteenth century) and proceeded to stock the abbey ponds with excellent carp, which they fished for by way of recreation and ate for dinner in the fasting seasons. Those of the family who took Holy Orders, brought up from infancy to this pastime, continued to practice it assiduously in the various pleasant livings which came their way. One of them, rector of East Harting in the late eighteenth century, wrote in his journal (published in 1810) that he prepared most of his sermons while thus engaged; he thought that his vocation as fisher of men was assisted by miming it out on the riverbanks, and each fish that he landed caused him to exult greatly, as if he had captured a soul. When they nibbled at the bait, he prayed; when they got away, he repented of his own unworthiness that caused his hand to fail, and took it as divine correction. Subsequently he became a bishop but did not cease to fish.[12]

One of Laurie's ancestors, she notes, became a Roman Catholic and, afterward, caught only very tiny fish. With such bad luck, he cried out,

> "Church of my baptism! Why did I ever leave you?" [and so] returned to his spiritual home and was presently rewarded by a miraculous draught of fishes in Loch Tay. Which, as my aunt Dot said, just showed.[13]

This reminds me of the suggestion that Izaak Walton's *Compleat Angler* might be read as *Compleat Anglican.*[14]

Later in Macaulay's story, Aunt Dot and Father Pigg wander into Russia, where they are arrested as spies. Meanwhile, Laurie rides off to Palestine on the white camel, finally returning to England, along with her dromedary, onboard a shipping vessel. It's a delightful book and funny—especially to readers acquainted with American Episcopalianism.

12. Macaulay, *Towers of Trebizond,* 5–7.

13. Macaulay, *Towers of Trebizond,* 8.

14. So James Prosek, fishing-book author and illustrator, suggests in his podcast on YouTube (wayupstream1, "Complete Angler").

Now consider tall tales about fishing, they being what most people think that anglers usually tell. Such is behind the verse

Early to bed
Early to rise
Fish all day
Make up lies!

One might suppose that fishing tall tales are many, but, evidently, most have not been recorded for posterity. A Google search found only a few book titles that suggested that they might have a "Paul Bunyan and Babe the Blue Tuna"-like account in them. One is *The Everything Tall Tales, Legends and Other Outrageous Lies*, compiled by Nat Segaloff, but it carried only a single uninteresting story about the Loch Ness monster. A book with more promise—and a long title—is *Incredible—and True!—Fishing Stories: Hilarious Feats of Bravery, Tales of Disaster and Revenge, Shocking Acts of Fish Aggression, Stories of Impossible Victories and Crushing Defeats*. Author Shaun Morey traveled to Alaska, Australia, Mexico, and the Caribbean to interview anglers, boat captains, guides, and witnesses who could say, "Yes, such and such really happened!" One account tells of a daredevil who leapt from a helicopter onto the back of a marlin and rode it rodeo-style. Another tells of catching a whopping 3,001 bass in a single summer season on Long Island, and a third shares the story of a grueling 37-hour fight with a Pacific salmon. All the stories are professed to be true. As tall tales, however, these still don't match up to Mark Twain's "The Celebrated Jumping Frog of Calaveras County" or Edward O'Reilly's "Saga of Pecos Bill"—Bill, who lassoed a tornado. One might have hoped for an angling tale of walking across a river on the back of salmon "stacked up like cordwood," or one about an osprey who carries a fishless lad to a trout-rich cirque lake, or a story about a "kindly Northern" who pulls a boat to a secret cove holding three-foot walleyes . . . or something like that. But no. There is little, tall-tale material to be easily found. The reader will need to go back to Chapter 2 of this book, "Fables," to find fish stories of the fantastical variety.

Even so, a 2008 edition of *The Farmer's Almanac* had a contest to find the best tall tales and fishing stories. The two below were prizewinners:

> [A man fishing near a lake spotted] a grey squirrel in the trees near the shore. The tree limbs hung over the lake. In the lake was a stump with two nuts on it. The squirrel was desperately trying all of his acrobatic gyrations in an effort to reach the nuts. Just as he

> grabbed them, he lost his grip and fell into the water. Instantly the biggest fish the man had ever seen lunged up and swallowed the squirrel. The lake got calm again. Then the big fish jumped up out of the water and put the two nuts back on the stump.[15]

> According to a 2003 news report, two workers in New York City's New Square Fish Market—one a Christian, the other a Jew—said they were about to kill a carp to be made into gefilte fish when the fish began shouting at them in Hebrew The Jewish fishmonger translated the fish's message as, "Everyone needs to account for themselves because the end is nigh." He said the fish went on to identify itself as the soul of a local Hasidic man who had died the previous year and instructed him to pray and study the Torah. Though shocked by the fish's loquaciousness, the workers ultimately opted to kill the fish and sell it anyway.[16]

Another who imagined the possibility of a talking fish was 19th-century essayist and poet Leigh Hunt, who included a human-piscine exchange in his poem "To a Fish/A Fish Answers." First, a human speaks derisively to a fish:

> To a Fish
> You strange, astonished-looking, angle-faced,
> Dreary-mouthed, gaping wretches of the sea,
> Gulping salt-water everlastingly,
> Cold-blooded, though with red your blood be graced,
> And mute, though dwellers in the roaring waste;
> And you, all shapes beside, that fishy be—
> Some round, some flat, some long, all devilry,
> Legless, unloving, infamously chaste:
> O scaly, slippery, wet, swift, staring wights,
> What is't ye do? What life lead? eh, dull goggles?
> How do ye vary your vile days and nights?
> How pass your Sundays? Are ye still but joggles
> In ceaseless wash? Still naught but gapes, and bites,
> And drinks, and stares, diversified with boggles?

> A Fish Answers
> Amazing monster! that for an aught I know,
> With the first sight of thee didst make our race
> Forever stare! O flat and shocking face,
> Grimly divided from the breast below!
> Thou that on dry land horribly dost go

15. Boeckmann, "Taller-Than-Typical Tales!"
16. Kilgannon, "Miracle? Dream? Prank?"

With split body and more ridiculous pace,
Prong upon prong, disgraced of all graces,
Long-useless-finned, haired upright, unwet, slow!
O breather of unbreathable, sword-sharp air,
How canst exist? How bear thyself, thou dry
And dreary sloth? What particle canst share
Of the only blessed life, the watery.
I sometimes see of ye an actual pair
Go by! linked fin by fin! most odiously.[17]

Now another humorous fishing-story form—jokes. Jokes are invariably told around fishing lodges and streamside campfires. They appear on bait-shop tack boards and fly-shop plaques. The first fishing joke that I ever heard was an ecumenical one. It starts out, "A priest, a preacher and a rabbi went lake-fishing together."

> After a while, the priest needed to go to shore. So, he stepped out of the boat, walked across the water like Jesus, and came back. The rabbi was amazed. Soon, the preacher did the same shore-and-back routine. Ultimately, the rabbi decided he might try it himself, so he stepped out—and sank to his chest. The preacher turned to the priest and said, "Guess we should have shown him where the rocks are."

To that early joke, I've added many more to my repertoire, like those below, offered in shortened form.

> A kid was catching fish in freezing weather and was asked by unsuccessful fishers what he was using. He didn't reply. Asked again, he still didn't answer. On the third request, the lad finally spit out into his hand and confessed, "Worms!"
>
> The game warden discovers a woman in a boat, reading a book in a quiet cove. He accuses her of fishing without a license. She protests, but he says evidence of fishing is there in all the equipment in the boat. She says, "If you arrest me, I'll charge you with statutory rape." "But I haven't touched you," the warden says. "True, but you have all the equipment."

17. Hunt, "To a Fish/A Fish Answers."

> One mayfly said to another during their hatch, "We have 24 hours to mate, lay eggs, and die . . . and now you tell me you're just not into me!"
>
> Fishermen in a coastal village in Maine weren't sure about taking their new Methodist minister, a woman, fishing, as they had previous-serving male clergy. But they did, and she met them Monday morning at the dock. Starting out of the harbor, they realized they'd left their bait behind. She said, "I'll get it," and walked on the water for the retrieval, causing one fisherman to comment, "Isn't that just like the bishop! Sent us someone who can't swim."
>
> A man, reluctant to fish with dynamite as his friends had, was, nevertheless, given a lighted stick and asked, "Well, are you gonna fish or just sit there?"
>
> Sven and Ollie had a great day catching. To remember their excellent fishing location, Sven put a big "X" in the bottom of their rental boat. "Good idea," said Ollie, "but what if, next time, we don't get the same boat?"
>
> The owner of a fly shop in Idaho was giving directions to a fishing spot to a customer from New York. "Take the first two-track on the left after you pass the cattle guard," the shop owner said. The New Yorker thanked him and started for the door, then turned and asked, "What kind of uniform does a cattle guard wear?"

Here's one claimed to be one of the best fishing jokes, a blonde joke:

> Three blondes are sitting by the side of a river holding fishing poles with the lines in the water. A game warden comes up behind them and says, "Excuse me, ladies, I'd like to see your fishing licenses." "We don't have any," replied the first blonde. "Well, if you're going to fish, you need fishing licenses," said the game warden. "But officer," replied the second blonde, "we aren't fishing. We all have magnets at the end of our lines, and we're collecting debris off the bottom of the river." The game warden lifted up all the lines, and, sure enough, there were horseshoe magnets tied on the end of each line. "Well, I know of no law against it," said the game warden. "Take all the debris you want." And, with that, he left. As soon as the man was out of sight, the three blondes started laughing hysterically. "What a dumb fish cop," the second blonde said to the other two, "doesn't he know that there are steelhead in this river?!"

The most recent fishing joke I've heard goes like this:

> There once was a Texan who came to Colorado and hired a guide to take him fishing. On the water, the Texan was bothered by buzzing insects and finally asked, "What are these anyway?" The guide said, "They're zoom-zoom flies." "Zoom-zoom flies? Never heard of 'em." The guide explained: "They usually hang around horses' asses." The Texan then demanded, "Are you calling me a horse's ass?" "Oh, no, sir, not me, but you can't fool a zoom-zoom fly."

The number of fishing jokes is seemingly endless. I found this one hanging in an Ontario, Canada, fly-in outpost:

Men and fish are alike
They get in trouble
When they open their mouths!

Assuredly, there is much angling humor in cartoons. One *Far Side* cartoon—perhaps my favorite—shows two guys in a boat with mushroom-shaped nuclear clouds rising up behind them, one guy saying to the other, "I'll tell you what it means, Norm. No size regulations and screw the limits."

Here's a description of another cartoon: Two bears are sitting at a dining table, about to order dinner. One bear says to the other, "Remember, Boris, red wine goes with hunters, but white wine goes with fishermen."

Before bringing this chapter to a close, mention must be made of a humorous short film with a fishing theme. It is Laurel and Hardy's 1932 classic *Towed in a Hole*. The scenes focus on the pair's zany attempts to get their old car to a fishing location. The audience is left laughing at their futile attempts. Fishers will laugh, remembering, "In my old chariot, I've been there, done that."

The above is enough to fix humor—in books, written stories, tall tales, jokes, cartoons, and movies—as a distinct genre within the angling corpus. Humor is also regularly found within the genre that I call angling adventure stories, which are covered in the next chapter of this book.

One additional word about humorous fishing literature—and perhaps all varieties of humor: Something true, often profound, may be found within the humor. Even fishing humor sometimes includes what sociologist of religion Peter Berger calls "signals of transcendence," which point to truths about human limitations and foibles, relationships (especially male-female), and life beyond death.

Chapter 12

Angling Adventure Essays

After considering cultural tales, fables, biblical stories, classic literature, existential and spiritual offerings, outlier sources, informational and instructional contributions, children's stories, poems, songs, and angling humor, we come to the final genre of fishing-fish-and-water literature, the angling adventure essay.

Typically, this genre of story is a first-person narrative that is a true tale of a fishing trip taken with a friend or guide. On such excursions, things—incidents, accidents, learnings, and luck (good or bad)—occur that mark the trip as an adventure. Characters often engage in spirited banter; fishers share their angling insights. The best stories are well-crafted, informative, and often humorous. Pen-and-ink drawings or other art, even charts, regularly accompany the essays. In glossy-page publications, high-resolution color photographs appear. As to length, that will vary, say, from 2,000 to 7,000 words. It is more useful, however, to think in terms of "time to read." The usual short angling tale is one that can be read in a single sitting, as master of the short story, Edgar Allen Poe, suggests. The short angling adventure story may be a stand-alone piece, but it also could be part of a collection of stories by the same author or bundled with stories by other writers into an anthology.

The mystery writer and fisher Mary Roberts Rinehart gives an account of her family's 1916 trip to Glacier National Park that is representative of a short angling adventure story. Her account includes this riveting recollection:

> I have still in mind a deep pool where the water, rushing at tremendous speed over a rocky ledge, fell perhaps fifteen feet. I had fixed my eyes on that pool early in the day, but it seemed impossible to access. To reach it, it was necessary again to scale a part of the cliff, and, clinging to its face, to work one's way round along a ledge perhaps three inches wide. When I had once made

it, with the aid of friendly hands and a leather belt, by which I was lowered, I knew one thing—knew it inevitably. I was there for life. Nothing would ever take me back over that ledge.

However, I was there, and there was no use wasting time. For there were fish there. Now and then they jumped. But they did not take the fly. The water seethed and boiled, and I stood still and fished, because a slip on that spray-covered ledge and I was gone, to be washed down to Lake Chelan, and lie below sea-level in the Cascade Mountains. Which might be a glorious sort of tomb, but it did not appeal to me.

I tried different flies with no result. At last, with a weighted line and a fish's eye, I got my first fish—the best of the day, and from that time on I forgot the danger.

Someday, armed with every enticement known to the fisherman, I am going back to that river. For there, under a log, lurks the wiliest trout I have ever encountered. In full view he stayed during the entire time of my sojourn. He came up to the fly, leaped over it, made faces at it. Then he would look up at me scornfully.

"Old tricks," he seemed to say. "Old stuff—not good enough." I dare say he is still there.[1]

The short angling essay often appears in sport magazines like *Field and Stream, Outdoor Life*, *Great Days Outdoors*, *Sports Afield*, and *Game & Fish*. These publications primarily feature hunting or fishing stories although you occasionally find a piece on skiing, hiking, or rock climbing. A recent issue of *Field and Stream* had a short story titled "Jump In." Here is an excerpt:

> From the bank, I pulled the knot tight on my dropper fly and looked out over the river, which sent a quick shiver of fear knifing through my excitement, like the feeling you have before you get on a carnival ride. The river was up, hurtling foam over the boulders after one of those long summer rainstorms that leaves wisps of steam spiraling about the fields–exactly how it looked when my grade-school buddy Jo and I first fished the spot, years ago.
>
> Jo had a reputation as a tough kid. (Nobody pointed out to Jo, for example, that only girls spell that name without the e.) The river didn't scare him. He hiked the worm box—filled

1. Rinehart, *Tenting To-Night*, 144–45.

> with the night crawlers we'd pinched in the rain the night before—from his waist to his armpits and cinched the belt across his chest. Then he dropped in and battled the current to a rock below a roaring plunge pool.
>
> It was when he turned and motioned for me to wade in that his sneakers began to slide, and he started flailing in vain to catch his balance. The worm box popped open. Night crawlers sailed. And in the boiling slick below, where the fat morsels plopped and raced downstream, a yellow slab rose and parted the surface.
>
> It was the biggest trout I'd ever seen.
>
> After that, I wasn't scared either. I jumped in and lobbed a crawler into the slot—and the brown crashed and bolted downstream. As I leaned into the fish, my sneakers shot in opposite directions, and I rode the current downstream, rod held high above the froth. But when I finally got my footing, the fish had broken off.
>
> Upstream, Jo was laughing. Since we were both soaked, we spent that day wading or swimming to the river's hardest-to-reach holes—and had one of the best days of summer fishing I can remember.[2]

The Winter 2020 issue of *Sports Afield* carries an essay called "Black Ops." It's about ice fishing on Granby Lake, Colorado. The author tells of taking a 43-inch lake trout on, of all things, a 10-inch hogy—a fly used for bluefin tuna!

In a 2021 issue of *Game & Fish* magazine, five tantalizing titles are present:

"Alaskan Abundance" (Kenai Peninsula salmon fishing)

"Purple Reign" (purple dry-fly patterns)

"Catching Cats" (channel catfish)

"Hot Steel" (summer steelheading)

"Go With the Flow on the Mo" (fishing the Missouri River)

"Go With the Flow on the Mo" begins with these words:

> Big water, big trout, and big crowds. That's a fairly good description of Montana's blue-ribbon reach of the Missouri River between Helena and Great Falls. . . .[3]

2. Hurteau, "Jump In," 14.
3. McKean, "Go With the Flow on the Mo," 67.

Andrew McKean goes on to describe the river's stretch below Holter Dam that carries 5,000 trout per mile. He gives these instructions on fishing it:

> [T]ry swinging big articulated streamers for the Missouri's largest rainbow and brown trout, which can easily go to 20 inches with some trophy specimens taping 24 inches. For browns, nighttime fishing with streamers can be gold. . . .[4]

Although informative, an angling adventure follows when the author tells about taking some of those big browns.

The most prestigious outdoor-life magazine is *Gray's Sporting Journal*, which describes itself as "the magazine for discerning sportsmen." It carries exceedingly literate writing. John Gierach and Roderick Haig-Brown, among other luminaries, have had articles in *Gray's*. Some of the magazine's stories were collected into a book, *Tales From Gray's: Selections From Gray's Sporting Journal, 1975–1985*. Below is a summation of two of the fishing tales in the book.

"The View From Over the Hill" by Charles F. Waterman is an account by an aging angler that tells of his difficulties with eyesight (which difficulty I share), his piscatorial success, and his sagacious ruminations.

> A drop of sweat slipped down from my big hat and got into my eye, taking with it some of the sun screening lotion I have to wear these days. I've used up my tolerance to the sun and every year I have to go to a skin specialist who freezes off the cancerous little lesions caused by the sun exposure. Anyway, when the sun screening lotion gets into my eye it hurts. I have to wash it out pretty quick. When I tell young people about this sun trouble, they listen politely. I was up to my waist, and I saw a pink-sided rainbow rise in a little swatch of flat water between the rocky bank and a noisy boulder out near the middle. I still had the little Elk Hair Caddis and I false-casted it dry and then dropped it two feet above where I'd seen the last rise.
>
> It landed like a real caddis that time. The rainbow took it trustingly and I felt pretty good about the whole thing. I released the fish, stopped fishing and sloshed back to the truck with more trout rising. It was three hours until dark and my friend would have a great evening, coming in grinning as the light faded. I took off my waders and dried out, hearing a rising trout gurgle just over the bank. Pretty good day. Should sleep pretty well after we get home. The low sun gleamed on mountain snow, and I could see a little thunderstorm between some peaks.

4. McKean, "Go With the Flow on the Mo," 67.

> This is how you get old and if it's not good enough for you, you may do some hard time. Has this ruined your day?[5]

Another of *Gray's* excellent stories is "Not Rocking the Boats" by David James Duncan, author of *The River Why.* The story, while fictitious ("names changed to protect the innocent—or guilty") is totally plausible and true in sentiment with understandable anger and good humor. It begins this way:

> I intend never to write a How-to piece on fishing. My reason for this is simple. It stands 6-foot-six in hip boots, weighs two hundred and forty flabless pounds, has flaming red hair and huge red hands, and is prone to sudden outbursts of violence. Its name is Jeremiah Ransom. His friends call him "Jer."
>
> Jeremiah Ransom is a militant. His cause is flyfishing. And his principal political thesis is that the How-to Fishing Piece is the most overdone, formulaic, unconscionable branch of sporting literature in the world today, rivaling grocery store romances, novels about novelists, quick money and slow sex manuals, and Rajneesh books on the all-time Literary List of Paper-Wasters.
>
> How-to fishing pieces come in two sizes: the article, and the book. My friend Jeremiah's opinion of which of the two is worse seems to depend entirely on which of the two he has most recently been reading. He maintains, however, that the "Flyfishing Cognescenti" (i.e. he and his buddies) unanimously agree that in either form the only beneficiaries of the scrivening How-to-ists are the scriveners themselves, the fishing tackle industry, and the hordes of wild-flower-stomping, water-whacking rubes they lure to the riparian. The Cognescenti also agree that the How-to-ers' victims are untrammeled waters, fishermen who love solitude, the literature of fishing, and, of course, the fish.
>
> Ransom divides all How-to fishing writing into two categories: "redumbdancies," and "traitor tales." He claims the redumbdancy is the more common form, better measured in raw tonnage ("like sewage") than by lists of titles. These are the books and magazine articles that tirelessly plagiarize or rediscover—in English that gets progressively worser—all of the stalest, most rudimentary angling advice known to man. Jeremiah speculates that were the nation's top ten fishing writers to swap jobs with, say, the top ten basketball reporters, NCAA and NBA coverage would suddenly scintillate with titles like "How To Make Layups," "How To Jump," "How To Handle Those Pesky New Velcro Shoe-Fasteners," "How Tall Fast Players Are Often Preferable To

5. Charles F. Waterman, "The View From the Hill," in Gray, *Tales From Gray's*, 136–37.

> Short Slow Ones," "Some Advantages Of Outscoring The Opponent," and so on. His point, though a trifle overstated, is well taken.[6]

Later, the faux author (bearing similarities to Duncan himself) continues,

> "What should be done about these 'traitors'?" I once, innocently, asked my friend.
>
> "Two things," he replied. "One, boycott 'em: don't buy their books, magazines, rods, or flies, don't patronize their bloody shops or flycasting schools or guide services, don't join their private clubs, don't even look at their damned catalogs. And two: rock 'em."
>
> "Rock 'em?" I said blankly. Being something of a pacifist by habit, if not by intention, I was a long way from guessing what he meant.
>
> He nodded. "Most famous Western flywaters are big, so most famous traitors fish them from drift boats. Look in the magazines, find out what they look like, watch for 'em . . . and when you see one float by, rock him!"
>
> "Rock him?" It still hadn't sunk in.
>
> He nodded again. "Biggest damned rock you can throw! Aim for their writing hands! Aim for their cameras! Scare the feces out of 'em! They won't be back."
>
> I finally got it.[7]

So, the title of this story. It goes on from here to report that a flotilla of rafts comes by while the narrator, Ransom, and another friend are fishing the Deschutes River. Ransom, standing only on small pebbles—larger rocks not handy—screams curses at the outfitter, Jim Brennan. The outfitter, the oarsmen-guides, and the clients float on to set up camp below Ransom's.

Later that evening, Brennan, a fly-shop owner, photographer, and writer as well as an outfitter, comes by flashlight into Ransom and company's camp, offering a bottle of Jack Daniel's. After a round or two with it, Brennan turns to Jeremiah and asks, "What I came for, what I'd really like to know, is what you all—and especially you, Ransom—have against me." Then begins Ransom's speech:

> "What I have against you isn't much, Brennan. Only everything you've published, everything you say and do, every buck

6. David James Duncan, "Not Rocking the Boats," in Gray, *Tales From Gray's*, 191–92.

7. David James Duncan, "Not Rocking the Boats," in Gray, *Tales From Gray's*, 193.

> you make, everything you stand for. What I have against, you, Brennan. . . ."[8]

And he goes on in vitriol to list a half dozen more "what I have against you" complaints. At the end of Ransom's speech, Brennan, unperturbed, says, "Gosh, Jer, if that's all that's bothering you, heck! No problem!" Then, he smiles.

Others smile, even laugh, Jeremiah a little, and they pass the bottle till it's dry. At parting, Brennan invites Ransom to float-fish with him the next day. So,

> Jeremiah floated the river with Jim Brennan. He also accompanied him to Portland and to one of his "crapulous" fly shops, poked around the shelves, display cases and warehouse, took a peek at his books, talked with his employees and customers, and was moved by the whole experience to retract "maybe 15% of The Speech."[9]

Better than that, at the end of this tale, we learn Ransom now throws "about 25% fewer rocks"!

The greatest concentration of fly-fishing stories are found in publications singularly dedicated to the sport of fly fishing. The best-known nationally distributed magazines are *American Angler*, *Angler's Journal*, *Fly Fisherman*, *In-Fisherman*, *The Drake*, and *Trout*.

I had a story with photographs that appeared in a 1985 issue of *Fly Fisherman*. "Where the Big Fish Go . . . The Lower Gunnison River" is representative of the genre now under consideration.[10] I told the story of a three-day raft trip on Colorado's Gunnison River that I took with several fishing friends. Outfitter Gabe Magtutu led us, aided by three oarsmen-guides. I began the essay with a geologic description.

> The Black Canyon National Monument/Park has an "outer rim" and an "inner rim." The outer is of sandstones, hard whites at the very top, pinks of the Escalante formation underneath and, below that, reds of the Morrison. . . . We made our way off the

8. David James Duncan, "Not Rocking the Boats," in Gray, *Tales From Gray's*, 204.
9. David James Duncan, "Not Rocking the Boats," in Gray, *Tales From Gray's*, 208.
10. White, "Where the Big Fish Go," 44–45.

> outer edge down to the inner, finally to stand on metamorphic blocks 1.7 billion years old.[11]

There, a thousand feet below the rim, we met the guides, put our gear on board the rafts—that had been hauled in by horses the day before, along with tents and needed provisions—boarded the rafts ourselves, and began casting from the rafts.

> Al Heins [one friend on the trip] and I began fishing in a large eddy below the first rapids, where smooth water circled beside heavy bank grass. Spotting rises near the bank, I cast my fly, an irresistible, toward it, and a fat 12-inch brown promptly rose and took it. Al, using an elk hair caddis, soon had a little bigger brown. It was a taste of catchings to come.[12]

For the most part, we fished big nymphs below strike indicators. At one point on the second day, when Al and I learned that other anglers in our party had taken trout on the Rio Grande King, I suggested to our guide . . .

> that we switch to a dry. He then pointed to a nearby shore boulder, "Check that out." Atop it was the dry casing of a large stonefly. "That, Jim," he said, "is evidence of pteronarcys californica, America's largest stonefly, also known as the willow fly. They are," he continued, "big food for big trout. That's what we're after."
>
> ("Yes, of course," I remembered.)
>
> Gabe then demoed how to fish stonefly patterns. He would cast his weighted offering—without an indicator—three-quarters of the way upstream, let it sink, and drift down. Then slowly he'd twitch it back. I tried the technique through the afternoon with little catch and considerable re-rigging.
>
> The next day, [Bruce] Kuster [another friend on the trip] received similar instruction, AND had positive results. In one deep pocket his line stopped and suddenly a giant rainbow spirited out of the water, way into the air . . . and broke him off.
>
> Bruce's "Damn!" echoed off the canyon walls for miles. Seeing the fish come out, Magtutu commented, "That baby was two feet, six pounds."[13]

11. White, "Where the Big Fish Go," 44.
12. White, "Where the Big Fish Go," 45.
13. White, "Where the Big Fish Go," 45.

Kuster's escapee was the largest trout seen but provided evidence of what was fabled to be there. Happily, wonderful "ordinaries" *were* taken, to wit:

> By five o'clock we were off the river, coming ashore at "T-Dyke," so named because a "T" in pegmatite intrusion was in the rock wall there. The area was a wide, grassy arroyo coming in from the northeast. Here Gabe and his guys started setting up camp. In front of our campsite's sandy bank was a long and flat island of stones, sand, and grass. Quiet water two to three feet deep ran on each side of the island, and, as the west canyon wall began to drape the river in shade, a mayfly hatch of major proportion came on. The hatch of big bugs soon became omnipresent, enticing hungry browns to the surface everywhere. Big Royal Wulffs, big Parachute Adams, and, of course, big Rio Grande Kings—to size #8, if you can believe it—were put onto the water, to be indiscriminately taken. It was the fastest fishing of the trip. E'er the dinner bell sounded, and darkness came on, in net count we all were reaching toward double digits.[14]

On this fishing trip, there was for me a "thin place," where I felt close to the divine:

> Our first night of camping was on a sandy left bank beneath immensely high rock walls, the walls separated by a little run-in canyon. As the guides put dinner together, I ventured up the draw to a high point for a photo of the canyon in some of its grandeur. The walls, the spires, the different colored rocks—oxidized red granites, white and black banded schist, white veined intrusions into dark and light gray gneiss, all of it mixed up, crunched, and roughed up—brought "spectacular" to a whole new level. Above was a cerulean blue sky, punctuated by white-foam clouds in gentle drift. The sound of the cascading river and of the wind whistling up the canyon made organ chords, so I thought.
>
> Then it hit me: Self, you are in no ordinary setting, but a vertical wilderness sanctuary, God's primordial cathedral. To Hagia Sophia in Constantinople and St. Peter's in Rome, I whispered, "Eat your heart out," then scribbled a wee prayer in my notebook: "Creator God, may your beauty, revealed in this cathedral, reside a little in me."[15]

14. White, "Where the Big Fish Go," 45.
15. White, "Where the Big Fish Go," 45.

The Black Canyon of the Gunnison story ends with these words:

> That evening as the western sky was fading orange to indigo, all the piscators were making their way to their homes. We were pleased with the fishing, the camping and cuisine, the rafting, and the camaraderie—not to forget, great weather. A most awesome and satisfying three days.
>
> And one more word about the fishing for me. It is this: after three decades of dreaming Gunnison Black Canyon, I, at least, now know "where the big fish go to elude."[16]

I must say I was happy to have my stand-alone story told in *Fly Fisherman*. Month after month, year after year, for almost 50 years, other angling accounts have been presented in that national publication.

The organization Trout Unlimited also has a national publication—*Trout*. Besides articles focusing on cold-water conservation and news from and about TU chapters, there also are excellent stories. One such is by Dave Whitlock, fly-tyer extraordinaire, watercolorist, and angling sage. He has an article in the 2021 issue of *Trout*. It is called "Nymphin' for Deschutes Redbands." In this story—which looks back to the 1970s—Whitlock tells of traveling with his 12-year-old son, Joel. They fished waters in Colorado and Yellowstone, went to San Francisco (where Dave spoke), and, eventually, camped on Oregon's Deschutes River. There, while all other anglers were fishing dry flies—mostly unsuccessfully—Dave and his son went to indicator nymphing, not often practiced at the time, resulting in this account:

> We were on the last river section before taking out to camp. As we floated over the riffle, I saw at least a dozen larger redbands [rainbows] just below the riffle. I helped Joel wade out knee deep into a fine-looking riffle-run interchange. From his recent practice on Yellowstone's rivers, he knew how to present a 25-foot cast up and across the current, how to mend—and how to react to the indicator. On about his fifth presentation, with our guide at my shoulder as we were watching his indicator intently, it abruptly stopped. Joel reacted immediately with a brisk rod tip response and the next thing we saw was his backing and what looked like a leg-long rainbow tail walking. It turned out to be a 21-inch redband: the longest landed that day among our four-boat group. I was so darned proud of him and how he caught it. Joel hooked three more before we had to row to our riverside campsite.[17]

16. White, "Where the Big Fish Go," 45.
17. Whitlock, "My Favorite Trout Experiences," 67–68.

The piece includes a beautiful Whitlock watercolor of a Deschutes redband.

As stated, Whitlock's essay with others, appeared in *Trout*. Other countries, it must be noted, have dedicated fishing journals of their own. *Trout and Salmon* is a British publication. *Scale* is published in Germany. *Lure* covers European waters broadly, and there is *Outdoor Canada*. Other magazines around the world regularly carry short fishing stories, freshwater and "of the salt." It is hard to imagine Norway or South Africa, Argentina, or Japan without such offerings.

Returning to the United States, we have regional fishing journals: *Northwest Fly Fishing*, *Southwest Fly Fishing*, *Eastern Fly Fishing*, and *Southern Culture on the Fly*.

In America, the divisions of parks, recreation, and wildlife of most states publish a monthly, quarterly, or annual magazine. *Colorado Outdoors* and *Wyoming Wildlife* are the two with which I am most familiar. Skipping around the four corners of the continental United States, one finds . . .

Maine Fish and Wildlife Magazine
Florida Wildlife Magazine
Alaska Fish and Wildlife News
California Outdoor

The California publication describes its pages with these words: "Compelling stories on the state's native species and habitat, presented with page after page of beautiful photographs."[18] That description could be used to represent the offerings of most states' outdoor publications.

The Colorado Parks and Wildlife Division, the agency that publishes *Colorado Outdoors*, issued this report on the taking of a state-record-breaking brook trout:

> A Colorado man has broken the state record for the largest brook trout ever reeled in. Matt Smiley, of Lake City, caught the fish last month in Hinsdale County. Officials with Colorado Parks and Wildlife sent out a news release on Tuesday with a photo of Smiley with the fish. It weighed in at 8 pounds and 9 ounces and was 26.25 inches long and had a girth of 16 inches. Smiley caught the fish in Waterdog Lake, which is on the east side of Lake City in the Uncompahgre National Forest at an elevation of just above 11,000 feet. The longtime fisherman described the

18. Statement extracted from https://wildlife.ca.gov/Publications/Outdoor-California.

> "experience of this catch" as surreal. He said the fish put up quite a fight, including jumping out of his net at one point.
>
> "She pulled and rolled and was doing crazy things," he said.
>
> After he caught the brook trout, Smiley hiked back to Lake City with it in his backpack and soon after had it weighed by a CPW aquatic biologist, and the new state record was certified.
>
> "The toughest thing for me with this whole deal was deciding to keep the fish. I've released so many over the years, but it was one of those deals where I made a quick decision and wanted to give this fish the recognition it deserves," he said in a prepared statement. This is the third time in 2022 that the state's brook trout record has been broken. The record had previously held for 75 years. One of the previous record-breaking catches was also made at Waterdog Lake.[19]

High Country Angler is Trout Unlimited's magazine for the Rocky Mountain West. Many of its stories are about fishing in Colorado. Illustrative of its content is "The Miraculous Draught of Fishes," a story I wrote about indicator fishing, using bobbers out of pontoon boats on Antero Reservoir one Memorial Weekend. I went with my oft-fished-with friend Bruce Kuster. That there is fly-fishing technical information in it and that remarkable things happened—some simply the result of dumb luck—is fairly typical of the short angling adventure story. I retell my published story here, quoting some of it and condensing other parts of it.

> We launched from the Antero south side boat ramp and rowed out exactly 300 strokes. The water was glassy, the sky overcast. Anchors were dropped and rigs put into action. I dedicated one of my rods "for midges only" and the other "strictly callibaetis," two flies per fitting. I wanted to know which set-up might be the most taken. Bruce, fishing with only one fly per rig, said, "I'm going to change every second catch."
>
> Right away, bang-bang, he caught two beautiful bows on a size 12 Hebgen callibaetis, a fly we developed while fishing Montana's Lake Hebgen. Having succeeded with the Hebgen, he next put on a dark #12 hare's ear. It took two, bang-bang.
>
> "Okay, now how about a zug bug?" he asked without waiting for an answer. It worked for two more.[20]

19. Posted as a Fall 2022 story from the Colorado Parks and Wildlife. The story with accompanying photographs could be viewed for months afterward on Colorado Parks and Wildlife Division's website.

20. White, "Miraculous Draught of Fishes," 41.

Over the course of the day, Bruce and I successfully used the following patterns: the bead head prince, a zebra midge, red annelid, purple San Juan worm, orange and yellow eggs, callibaetis (brown and black), frost-bite midge, golden stone, something called a "chromie," and I don't know what all. *Anything* put down to 11 feet worked. We could have used a dry fly, such as the Adam's, and hooked up.

Bruce and I doubled many times. We doubled ourselves individually when both our rigs were taken and, once, had four fish on at the same time, to net two. One fish-fighting episode in the larger narrative is this:

> The indicator on my midge rod suddenly disappeared in earnest. I lifted and felt that wonderful "solid something" on the other end.
>
> "It's a better one," I announced.
>
> The fish, first of all, dived deep and then started out on a long run, taking me, well into the backing. Could he be foul-hooked? Possibly. Eventually the strong-runner turned and passed under my pontoons. As he did, I saw that he held a fly in his chops. Then came an abrupt reverse and the showing of a yellow flash.
>
> I shouted, "I have a brown!"
>
> "Take him slow," Bruce called out.
>
> I would have, but he went screaming out again, stronger this second time and again exposing the white nylon backing beneath the floating yellow line. It was only with slow "lift rod up/pump down" handling that the fish returned.
>
> "This is indeed a bigger one."
>
> And he was. When I finally got him into the net and could measure him, he was a full twenty inches and, oh, so thick and deep. Likely four pounds.[21]

Here's how I ended the essay:

> With the wind picking up from the south, we had a challenging 600-stroke row back to the boat ramp. Once seated in the Tahoe, Bruce's boat within the vehicle and mine on top of it, I asked, "How many do you suppose you netted today?"
>
> "I'd say sixty, plus or minus. You?"
>
> "Fifty range. A biblical 'miraculous draught'."
>
> Actually: best catching day we've ever had in fifty years angling together. I mark it "Memorable Memorial Weekend."[22]

21. White, "Miraculous Draught of Fishes," 43.

22. White, "Miraculous Draught of Fishes," 44.

Some fishing publications are species-specific, e.g., *Bassmaster*, the magazine that distributes to a half-million anglers. Among other species-specific periodicals are *Crappie*, *Marlin*, *Musky America*, and *Total Carp*.

A recent issue of *Steelheader's Journal* carries a story of winter fishing on the Skeena River in British Columbia that serves as a representative short angling tale in a species-specific magazine. The story is called "The Last American Steelheader in Terrace." Though it was late in the season, author Brett Gaba and guide Gill Mckean (of West Coast Fishing Adventures) believed monster steelhead were still to be found. They worked their way up the river to a bend with a root wad in it. Gaba let his streamer drift toward the wad, receiving these instructions:

> "If you feel it take, put the cork to it right away: they'll break you off in here with all this wood," said Gill. As if on cue the line went tight as it got close to the root ball and I felt the shake and pulse of a good Canadian fish. It stayed in the soft water for a moment before charging upstream, quickly changing its mind, and bearing downstream with stately authority. I bent my rod towards the bank and tried to slow it down but there was simply no control in it. After just a few seconds, the line just went slack. The entire moment might have lasted 10 seconds. Gill and I looked at each other with the tell-tale shock and disbelief that passed between guide and sportsman after losing a good fish. I reeled up and looked at my fly, still mostly new in perfect condition after only a handful of casts but the thick hook was nearly straightened. "I would have liked to have gotten a better look at that fish, but I think we proved what we wanted to prove," he said. From there we worked our way down to the pool where we had spooked two fish on our way in, but we passed through without a take. At that point, the light winter sun was starting to weaken so we started walking back to the truck.[23]

Besides appearing in periodicals, the short fishing story may be part of a collection by an individual author. Bruce Ducker's book *Home Pool: Stories of Fly Fishing and Lesser Passions* is illustrative of a single-author collection.

23. Gaba, "Last American Steelheader," 89–90.

So is Robert Traver's *Trout Madness*. Likewise are the books by John Gierach that we shall come to shortly.

The North American "dean of fly fishing," Roderick Haig-Brown, has his essays assembled in *A River Never Sleeps* and *Fisherman Summer*. Here are two stellar quotes from them:

> There will be days when the fishing is better than one's most optimistic forecast, others when it is far worse. Either is a gain over just staying home.

and

> I still don't know why I fish or why other men fish, except that we like it and it makes us think and feel.[24]

Former President Jimmy Carter has collected his fishing and hunting stories in the book *An Outdoor Journal: Adventures and Reflections*. In it, he tells about fishing in a Georgia swamp and of a city woman who visited and worried that her child might drown there. A local fisherman assured her, however, "No child has ever drowned here—the alligators got 'em first!"[25]

One other prominent fishing author whose stories appear in a single volume is Thomas McGuane. His signature book is *The Longest Silence*. If some graphic artists' pieces are "*paint*erly," McGuane's prose can be said to be "*author*ially." He can be ranked right there with Hemingway and Maclean. His accounts, though, are never fiction but actual fishing adventures, masterfully told and totally believable. He is peerless in his description of fresh- and saltwater casting, the movement of rivers and seas, flora and fauna (from mango blossoms to tarpon scales), high Montana run-offs, Gulfstream deeps, friends fished with (musician Jimmy Buffett, writer Jim Harrison, and renowned fly fisherman George Anderson among others), personal ruminations, and much more. After reading McGuane's classic, other fishing writers could well say, "He's used up all the good words."

The Longest Silence contains 33 essays from 30 years of McGuane's worldwide travels. The titular "long silence" refers to the long time—many years—one has to wait for a hookup with a permit, a game fish of the western Atlantic Ocean. By means of exquisite description, McGuane takes the reader with him to catch Atlantic salmon in Russia, bonefish in Mexico, brown trout in Montana, steelhead in British Columbia, and tackle-busting tarpon in Florida. The taking of snook, stripers, and snappers are told as well as a fight with a marlin.

24. "Roderick Haig-Brown Quotes."

25. Carter, *Outdoor Journal*, heard on BARD.

Below are three excerpts from *The Longest Silence.* The first excerpt, not about fishing per se, reflects on angling's forefather, Izaak Walton. The passage reveals McGuane's literary, historical, and cultural depth.

> *The Compleat Angler* owes much of its interest to cycles of turbulence, starting with the one within which Walton wrote. In the years shortly before the Restoration, social discord, especially among the literate classes, rose to a genuinely dangerous level. The austerities of Cromwell were undertones of an ominously gathering future. Quietist dreaming, gentleness and contemplation, rusticity, and the ceremonies of country life, including fishing, beckoned compellingly. From the Restoration until now, *The Compleat Angler* has been renewed by turmoil, none more conspicuous than the Industrial Revolution, which produced an explosion in the popularity of angling and an idealization of the pastoral life.[26]

The second excerpt, from his "Iceland" chapter, illustrates something of McGuane's delightful sense of humor.

> That night, I found myself dining with some English salmon anglers. One, a florid, lively man in his sixties, was telling me of the recent death of his mother who had always been bored by salmon fishing. On the Alta, where his father had persuaded her to fish for one day, she caught a fifty-pounder and never fished again. This year, as she lay on her deathbed, her son sat by her side. She was only occasionally conscious as her life ebbed away. At the end, she opened her eyes and gazed at him. "You'll never catch a fifty-pound salmon," she said, and died.[27]

The last McGuane quote is an extended excerpt appearing in the chapter "Sons," regarding fishing for permit in the Caribbean with his son Thomas:

> Pedro [their Mayan guide] stared in the direction he was poling, getting remarkable progress from the short hardwood crook with which he pushed us along. Pedro had a faint smirk on his face, as though reading my thoughts; more likely he was feeling that the hopelessness of predictably catching a permit was his own secret.
>
> The little bay had a bottom too soft for wading. We were at a relatively low tide and the hermit crabs could be seen clinging to the exposed mangrove root. "Palometta," Pedro said, and

26. McGuane, *Longest Silence*, 229.

27. McGuane, *Longest Silence*, 235.

we looked back to see which way his phenomenal eyes were directed. A school of permit was coming onto the sandbar that edged the flat. . . . I checked to see if I was standing on my line, then I held the crab fly by the hook between my left thumb and forefinger and checked the loop of line. We were closing the distance fast and the permit were far clearer than they had been moments before. The skiff ground to a halt in the sand. Pedro said that I was going to have to wade to these fish. Well, that was fine, but the few permits I have ever hooked wading had spooled me while I stood and watched them go. I climbed out; eyes locked on the fish.

"Dad!" came my son's voice, "I've got to try for these fish, too!"

"Thomas, dammit, it's my shot!"

"Let me give it a try!"

Now I was nearly in casting position, then heard something behind me. Thomas had bailed out of the boat and was stripping line from his reel. He was defying his father! Pedro was celebrating three thousand years of Mayan family life on this bay by holding his sides and laughing. For all I knew, he had suggested my son dive into the fray.

Once in casting range, I was able to make a decent presentation and the crab landed without disturbance in front of the school. They swam right over the top of it. They ignored it. Another cast, I moved the fly one good strip. They inspected it and again refused. A third cast and a gingerly retrieve. One fish peeled off, tipped up on the fly and ate. I hooked him and he seared down the flat a short distance, then shot back into the school. Now the whole bunch was running down the flat with my fish in their midst. Thomas waded to cut them off and began to false cast. I saw disaster staring at me as his loop turned over in front of the school and his fly dropped quietly.

"Got one!" he said amiably as his permit burned its way toward open water. Palming my whirling reel miserably, I realized why he had never been interested in a literary career. He instead would content himself with life. He seemed to be enjoying the long runs his fish made; mine made me ill. He was still in diapers when I caught my first permit but my anxiety over a hookup had never abated.

Pedro netted my son's fish, his first permit, and waited, holding it underwater until mine was landed. Thomas came over with the net. When the fish was close, I began to issue a stream of last-minute instructions about the correct landing of a permit. He just ignored them and scooped it up.

> This was unbelievable, a doubleheader on fly-caught permit. I was stunned. We had to have a picture. I asked Pedro to look in my kit for the camera. Pedro admitted that he had only had this happen once before. He groped deeper in my kit.
>
> But I had forgotten the camera, and when Thomas saw my disappointment, he grabbed my shoulders. He was grinning at me. All my children grin at me, as if I was crazy in an amusing sort of way.
>
> "Dad," he said, "it's a classic. Don't you get it?" He watched for it to sink in. "It's better without a picture."
>
> The permit swam away like they'd known all along that we weren't going to keep them.[28]

In a lesser league is my own multiple-stories-under-one-cover book, *Fly-fishing the Arctic Circle to Tasmania.* The following excerpt is from the chapter "Europe on the Fly, Learning To Fish Blind."

> Alerted to my vision problems, Martin [my Czech guide] put white Pulsa pinch-on indicators to my leader, not one but two, seven feet above the point fly. As a result I could sometimes see the indicators floating down. After several casts and drifts, I detected a take, lifted my rod, and hooked up. Turns out it was a nice rainbow, about a foot long, 30 cm. (I'm getting this metric stuff.) Later in the morning I got a second bow.
>
> Now, here's something quirky that happened. Preparing to cast upstream, I let my flies drop into the water, next to the bank behind me. In casting forward, I was suddenly hurling a small fish through the air. He had taken the fly just as I cast. It was a six-inch/15.24 cm chub, making me think, "An Izaak Walton fish in Bohemia." In truth, such fish are probably all over European waters. Not only did I catch a chub, but also, later, a dace.[29]

Later still, I caught a roach, a gudgeon, and a grayling, which, with the earlier bows and later browns, constitute what might be considered a "Czech grand slam."

Short accounts of angling adventures, penned by multiple authors, may be found in anthologies. Here are some titles:

Robert DeMott, editor, *Astream: American Writers on Fly Fishing*

28. McGuane, *Longest Silence*, 286–88.
29. White, *Fly-fishing the Arctic Circle*, 243.

Arnold Gingrich, editor, *American Trout Fishing*

Danielle J. Ibister, editor, *The Fly Fishing Anthology*

Nick Lyons, *The Best Fishing Stories Ever Told*

Nick Lyons, *The Gigantic Book of Fishing Stories*

Holly Morris, *A Different Angle: Fly Fishing Stories by Women*

David Profumo and Graham Swift, editors, *The Magic Wheel: An Anthology of Fishing Literature*

Gary Soucie, editor, *Home Waters: A Fly-fishing Anthology*

Lamar Underwood, *The Greatest Fishing Stories Ever Told: Twenty-Eight Unforgettable Fishing Tales*

These anthologies carry stories and essays by our best-known angling authors, classic to contemporary. Some writers appear in more than one anthology. Here is an alphabetical partial listing of the authors in several of the books shown above:

> John James Audubon, Dave Barry, Richard Brautigan, Joe Brooks, John Bryan, Lord Byron, Jimmy Carter, Grover Cleveland, John Gierach, Theodore Gordon, Zane Grey, Roderick Haig-Brown, Jim Harrison, Ernest Hemingway, James Henshall, Gerard Manley Hopkins, Washington Irving, Michael Keaton, Charles Kingsley, Rudyard Kipling, Lefty Kreh, Gary LaFontaine, Andrew Lang, Sydney Lea, Ted Leeson, Nick Lyons, Norman Maclean, Thomas McGuane, Harry Middleton, Paul O'Neil, James Prosek, Howell Raines, Lee Anne Schreiber, Ernest Schweibert, Hart Stilwell, Henry David Thoreau, Izaak Walton, Ted Williams, Joan Wulff, Lee Wulff, Ed Zern

. . . and more than 100 others if we pulled all the names from the anthologies.

Nick Lyons' *Gigantic Book* (almost 800 pages!) has classic tales, wonderful poems, humorous stories, and serious reflections, all accompanied with his own pen-and-ink drawings. Lyons includes his own essay "Brautigan's Trout." In it, he tells of the last fishing trip of novelist Richard Brautigan, author of *Trout Fishing in America*, and the car wreck that ended his life.[30]

Western novelist Zane Grey, author of *Riders of the Purple Sage*, has an essay on tarpon fishing in a Caribbean estuary. There, he almost lands a seven-footer. We read, "Then the water split with a hissing sound to let out

30. Lyons, *Gigantic Book*, 720–31. In the "Fishing Humor" chapter of this anthology, a much lighter angling account by Brannigan himself is given.

a great tarpon, long as a door, seemingly as wide, who shot up and up into the air." Reeling the monster in, Grey discovers his line had frayed to a single thread. At the last moment, it breaks, enabling the fish to escape.[31]

Washington Irving, famous for *The Legend of Sleepy Hollow*, wrote an essay called "The Angler" in which he brings back Izaak Walton's *The Compleat Angler* and describes a fishing companion clothed with all the accouterment for the water, as Don Quixote was clothed for tilting at windmills. His angling success is minimal, as revealed in the following passage:

> I hooked myself instead of the fish; tangled my line in every tree; lost my bait; broke my rod; until I gave up the attempt in despair, and passed the day under the trees, reading old Izaak; satisfied that it was his fascinating vein of honest simplicity and rural feeling that had bewitched me, and not the passion for angling.[32]

Henry Van Dyke, known for his Christmas story *The Other Wise Man*, has an account of a fisherman named Beekman, who set out to make his wife, Cornelia, a fisher with him. For years, his wife resists Beekman's efforts to get her to try angling. Then, on the evening of the last night of the season, she goes out with him.

> At precisely fifty minutes past eleven, Beekman reeled up his line, and remarked with firmness that the holy Sabbath day was almost at hand, and they ought to go in.
>
> "Not till I've landed this trout," said Cornelia.
>
> "What? A trout! Have you got one?"
>
> "Certainly, I've had him on for at least fifteen minutes. I'm playing him Mr. Parsons' way. You might as well light the lantern and get the net ready; he's coming in towards the boat now."
>
> Beekman broke three matches before he made the lantern burn; and when he held it up over the gunwale, there was the trout sure enough, gleaming ghostly pale in the dark water, close to the boat, and quite tired out. He slipped the net over the fish and drew it in—a monster.
>
> "I'll carry that trout, if you please," said Cornelia, as they stepped out of the boat; and she walked into the camp, on the last stroke of midnight, with the fish in her hand, and quietly asked for the steelyard.
>
> Eight pounds and fourteen ounces that was the weight. Everybody was amazed. It was the "best fish" of the year.

31. Zane Grey, "Byme-by-Tarpon," in Lyons, *Gigantic Book*, 311–14.
32. Washington Irving, "The Angler," in Lyons, *Gigantic Book*, 506–12.

After this triumph, Cornelia is hooked on fishing, and, thereafter, Beekman becomes her come-along ghillie. From the trout's point of view, Van Dyke's story is rightly called "A Fatal Success."[33]

John McPhee, author of *Coming to the Country*, tells his own marital story titled "They're in the River" about being late reporting home to his wife because he spent two-and-a-half hours fighting a four-and-three-quarter-pound roe shad.[34]

Another fishing anthology is *Astream* by Robert DeMott. A tale called "Donor" by Ted Leeson, author of *The Habit of Rivers*, is included and begins by referencing ancient Greek dramas wherein a god appears as the "donor" to help a protagonist in time of trouble. Leeson recalls a time, three decades earlier, when his younger brother died by suicide. The death was devastating, and he just wasn't getting over it. Not sure what to do, Leeson went fishing—despondently, to be sure. He went to a trout creek in his home state of Wisconsin, a stream shared with his brother in happier days. Leeson's heart, though, wasn't in it; he was too deeply depressed. As he stood in the water, listlessly casting, a voice on the bank asked, "How are you doing?"

He turned and replied, "Not well," not referring to the fishing.

The stranger then asked to see Leeson's rig. Upon inspection, the man took Ted back to his truck, re-fitted the rig with a lighter leader, made a present to him of three small nymphs, wished him luck, and went his way, never to be seen or heard from again.

Leeson returned to fishing, the catch not remembered, but the donor of the leader and the three flies never forgotten. The donor, like a Greek god, had rescued him, giving him a life-restoring gift—a new faith in humanity.[35]

Also in DeMott's anthology is a story by Pam Houston titled "In the Company of Men (Redux)." She tells of being at Interlochen in Northern Michigan and being invited by friends (in this case, hard-core male anglers) to go a-fishing. They went out post-midnight in 16-degree weather for steelhead. One fellow, casting in the dark, takes one. She, however, only gets stuck in the mud, ending up over-her-waders wet in the river, and must be rescued out. All of which she remembers fondly, especially valuing the testosterone-charged company.[36]

A full nod to distaff anglers is offered in Holly Morris' *A Different Angle: Fly Fishing Stories by Women*. Her anthology captures the bracing adventures and meditative moments of fishing in the words of 34 women

33. Henry Van Dyke, "A Fatal Success," in Lyons, *Gigantic Book*, 732–38.
34. John McPhee, "They're in the River," in Lyons, *Gigantic Book*, 125–27.
35. Ted Leeson, "Donor," in DeMott, *Astream*, 143–51.
36. Pam Houston, "In the Company of Men (Redux)," in DeMott, *Astream*, 111–19.

anglers. They go from teasing trout and salmon in the Pacific Northwest to chasing bass and catfish in America's Deep South. One story is a humorous piece by Pulitzer Prize-winning novelist E. Annie Proulx. In the dry-wit style of Patrick McManus, she tells the story "Somewhere With Sven." Here's how she begins it:

> The critical geometry in the camping trip is the other person. I am not a Type-A camper—more of a B minus—but my friend Sven, with whom I have tented for a decade, falls off the far end of the scale. Triple Z. His attitude would give a frisson of danger to a wienie roast in a state park. I swear each trip is the last, but back home, all cracked fingernails and gravel burns, I know I've been somewhere.[37]

One camping trip—purpose of fishing—involves Sven's tiny "fishing car," ever errant. On their trip, the car doesn't completely break down but sticks in second gear and grinds in third and fourth. Later, we learn the trouble is caused because Sven put motor oil in the transmission! Another time, Proulx and Sven, in order to drive the fishing car through a flooded road, dismantled a beaver dam, only to become hopelessly mired in mud. They never got around to fishing on that trip.[38]

A second story in Morris' book is "A Fly Fishing Life" by Joan Wulff. It traces her career as a dancer and fly-caster from childhood. As a young woman, encouraged by French hotelier and fly-fishing specialist Charles Ritz, Joan won international fly-casting tournaments. Here is description of her becoming "properly attired":

> In 1954 I did a series of shows in the Midwest with Monte Blue, star of the silent screen, as emcee. When I showed up in my shorts, hip boots, and creel, which was everyone's idea of a girl fisherman's costume, Monte took me aside and told me he wanted to try something different. "Wear a dress," he said, "a long one, and we'll wow 'em." Leaping at the chance to portray casting as feminine, I bought a strapless, ankle-length white dress with silver leaves on it, high-heeled sandals and, to complete the outfit, rhinestones for my hair. The combination was perfect in that Monte presented my act beautifully, speaking softly, while I was casting . . . in time with the music. "Up a Lazy River" was a natural, and the audiences responded. It couldn't last forever, though, and without either Monte or an orchestra the costume didn't play as well mixed in with lumberjacks, retrievers, and

37. E. Annie Proulx, "Somewhere With Sven," in Morris, *Different Angle*, 13.

38. E. Annie Proulx, "Somewhere With Sven," in Morris, *Different Angle*, 13–24.

> Sparky the Seal. I changed back to the shorts, boots, and creel outfit—but I'll remember the gown and music as being the perfect way to depict fly casting as an art form, especially suitable for women.[39]

There are other contributors to Morris' anthology, such as Lorian Hemingway (granddaughter of Ernest) and Lee Ann Schreiber. The book is an excellent and novel offering that must cause Dame Juliana Berners, who wrote *Fishing With an Angle* in 1496, to smile from her heavenly streambank.

Finally, among the angling anthologies is one from the 21st century: *The Fly Fishing Anthology,* compiled and edited by Danielle Ibister. Hers is a handsome coffee-table volume with beautiful full-page photographs, colorful art, and other graphics. It is divided into six major chapters, each with three or four essays by well-known writers. Chapter 3, "Fly Fishing Country," has accounts by John Gierach, Zane Grey, Ernest Hemingway, and Robert Traver. Grey's piece is titled "Colorado Trails." He recounts a time when he and his brother R. C. fished their beloved West in the early 1900s.

> These are educated trout," he said. "It takes a skillful fisherman to make them rise. Now anybody can catch the big game of the sea, which is your forte. But here you are N. G. [No Good?] . . . Watch me cast!"
>
> I watched him make a most atrocious cast with his double flying. But the water boiled, and he hooked two good-sized trout at once. Quite speechless with envy and admiration I watched him play them and eventually beach them. They were cutthroat trout, silvery-sided and marked with the red slash along their gills that gave them their name. I did not catch any while wading, but from the bank I spied one, and dropping a fly in front of his nose, I got him. R. C. caught four more, all about a pound of weight, and then he had a strike that broke his leader. He did not have another leader, so we walked back to camp.[40]

Stepping from angling adventure stories found in anthologies, we end this chapter reviewing books and articles by John Gierach.

For the title of this book, I have used John Gierach's surname, in part, for alliterative pairing with Gilgamesh, the ancient king of Babylon (written about in Chapter 1). Gierach is a 21st century C.E. person, while Gilgamesh

39. Joan Salvato Wulff, "A Fly Fishing Life," in Morris, *Different Angle*, 147–56.

40. Ibister, *Fly Fishing Anthology*, 71–72.

is of the 21st century B.C.E., so, in addition to providing alliteration, the names provide a bracketing of the time period spanned in this book's collection. In the more than 4,000 years separating Gilgamesh and Gierach, as we have seen, are too many fishing, fish, and water tales to recount.

Gierach is simply the master of the angling adventure essay. His stories are ever informative, lucid, witty, and insightful—"richly observant and wryly descriptive," as stated on the dust jacket of his book *Even Brook Trout Get the Blues*. Early on, he had stories in *The New York Times*, and, in recent years, he has contributed to *Trout*, the national journal of Trout Unlimited. In reviewing his books, the *Houston Chronicle* calls him "America's best fishing writer."[41]

Here are some of his evocative titles:

Trout Bum

The View From Rat Lake

Sex, Death, and Fly-fishing

Even Brook Trout Get the Blues

Where the Trout Are As Long As Your Leg

Dances With Trout

Another Lousy Day in Paradise

Standing in a River Waving a Stick

Death, Taxes, and Leaky Waders

At the Grave of the Unknown Fisherman

Still Life With Brook Trout

Fool's Paradise

No Shortage of Good Days

All Fishermen Are Liars

Dumb Luck and the Kindness of Strangers

All the Time in the World

Within each book are 20 or so essays, each 15 pages, more or less, in length. In *The View From Rat Lake*, Gierach explains what he hopes to do in his stories: "to tell the plain truth about fly-fishing and still be a humorist."[42] Gierach's truth has been learned from experiences with rivers, fellow fishers, flies and tackle, techniques, fish caught or released. He tells of his coffeepot,

41. Article from the Trout Unlimited website, "John Gierach."

42. Gierach, *View From Rat Lake*, 9.

truck of 200,000 miles, preference for split-bamboo rods, and bourbon of an evening with humor dry and wry.

Characteristically, Gierach takes the reader on a trip to someplace close (e.g., his backyard Saint Vrain Creek), distant (e.g., a remote river in Labrador), or somewhere in between—say, an Oklahoma farm pond. In *Trout Bum*, he writes, "Just to be on the road is good in a deep American way, but to be on the road going fishing is almost too good for words."[43]

Most often, Gierach travels in company with angling neighbors or fly-fishing superstars, like A. K. Best, Ed Engel, or Gary LaFontaine. With them, he goes high to a cirque lake for cutthroats or low to a tank in Texas for large-mouth bass. He reports their doings—successes, failures, foibles—and things seen, heard, "felt-n-smelt." Reading a Gierach essay, the outdoors person likely will think, "Been there, done that."

Gierach tells of one trip to the remote Kazan River in Canada's North-west Territories, a river that mostly runs between lakes. He and Wally Allen went there for grayling while other fishers in their party concentrated on lake trout. He and Allen caught grayling to three pounds—one of Allen's was something of a record. A get-your-attention-event happened on a rapid between lakes. Gierach hooked a big grayling and followed the fish down-river to the top of his waders only to realize that he could not back out. He knew that getting washed down and drowning was a real possibility. Alerted to Gierach's plight, his French-Canadian guide quickly motored up-river, circled Gierach—and his still-on fish—to swing back saying, "Climb in over the gunnel." Priorities firmly in place, John first handed over his rod before climbing aboard himself. Once in the boat, he fought and netted the fish. All's well that ends well, we might say, but, later, the guide took his clients to a shore hill. Here, they saw grave markers for two fishers who had not gotten out of the river alive![44]

In one essay, Gierach reports on a weeklong, expenses-paid fishing trip to Scotland to go after Atlantic salmon. He and five other sports writers fished there for a week and caught only one fish, with which they each posed for a picture.[45]

In *The View From Rat Lake*, "The Big Empty River" offers an account of Gierach fishing the Henry's Fork of Idaho's Snake River. About the Fork, he writes: "In all human experience there are only four metaphysical summits:

43. Gierach, *Trout Bum*, 222.

44. Gierach, *Trout Bum*, 75–82.

45. Gierach, *Dances With Trout*, 89ff.

Valhalla, Heaven, Nirvana, and the Green Drake hatch on the Henry's Fork."[46]

Typical of Gierach, he begins this story in travel, from Colorado across Wyoming to Idaho with A. K. Best, going slow in a gas-guzzling motorhome. They are on the Fork in late June and early July, a prime time for the hatches of green, brown, and gray drakes that surface then in huge numbers. Gierach reports that, between 10 in the morning and 3 p.m., the mayflies "come off like clockwork." So, the fish are up on 'em—and, some years, the seagulls "down on 'em." In the water, one may also discover blue-winged olive flies, mahogany mayflies, young pale-morning duns, flying ants, beetles, and workman-like caddis.

On this rich aquatic banquet, he tells us, rainbow trout feast, get fat, and grow long. Daily on the Fork, he and A. K. net fish 20 inches or better. The fish can be gulpers who move up a water seam to do a U-turn or chug out of sight. They also can be picky: One regular riser, pursued for several hours, refused all artificial bait. Giving counsel as he goes along, Gierach says that an effective way to fish the Fork is with a downstream cast, which puts the fly in *front* of the line, leader, and tippet.

Central to this particular essay is the attention that Gierach gives to "The Crowd," that is, the thousands of serious and competent fishers who come from all over the world to fish the Fork in season. Gierach says, "There was neoprene, Gore-Tex, and graphite from horizon to horizon, punctuated by rubberized canvas and the odd wheat-colored gleam of split cane."[47] The flies that A. K. and he brought weren't right for the river that year. So, Gierach says, they went to Mike Lawson's Fly Shop to buy more of the only currently working pattern, causing professional fly-tyer A. K. to lament, "I've tied twenty-five-hundred-dozen flies this year and it burns my ass to have to buy these!"[48]

To escape "The Crowd," Gierach and Best went far downriver where it is known to be brown-drake water. Brown-drake nymphs, he lets us know, are burrowers in river mud, distinct from up-river green drakes, who reside beneath rocks. The brown-drake duns, he says, look like "a huge bug as mayflies go and, although they hatch in the low light of dusk, you can clearly see them sitting on the water at 50 yards. They look like sailboats."[49]

One evening, coming off the river in the dark—A. K. already back at the truck—Gierach says that he

46. Gierach, *View From Rat Lake*, 11.

47. Gierach, *View From Rat Lake*, 14.

48. Gierach, *View From Rat Lake*, 16.

49. Gierach, *View From Rat Lake*, 17.

> . . . stepped on a pair of nesting cranes. Two of them. Four feet tall. I screamed bloody murder, fell on my back, and lay there for five minutes trying to let it sink in that I wasn't dead, it was okay, it was just dark, that was all. Back at the truck someone said, "Heard you yell. Thought you were eaten by a bear. We were just gonna divide up your stuff."[50]

Another year, Gierach and Best returned to the Henry's Fork in late August. That was when the callibaetis were coming off the water, but the hatches of fishermen had left. The two had the river to themselves. Their fly was a #16 callibaetis spinner and, better, a flying-ant pattern, presented to cruising fish. A. K. and Gierach each got into double digits on big fish. Walking out that evening, A. K. remarked, tongue-in-cheek, "That'll teach us to come in the off-season."

"Trout Bum" John Gierach

50. Gierach, *View From Rat Lake*, 19.

Since Gierach and Best finally got on the Henry's Fork when "The Crowd" was gone, Gierach called his essay "The Big Empty River," the title being a variation of Hemingway's "Big Two-Hearted River," discussed in Chapter 5.

Thirty years after his first book, Gierach is still offering readers wonderful fishing tales. Some appear in issues of *Trout* magazine. In 2023, Gierach published a book titled *All the Time in the World*. One chapter relates a day of fishing the Big Hole River in Montana. The following excerpt illustrates the author's enduring descriptive gifts utilized in telling a compelling fishing story.

> One day we drove far up the Big Hole to where the river was creek-sized and wadable, meandering across a wide, willowy valley ringed with mountains under a turquoise sky—a real Montana postcard. But the temperature was already in the 90s, presaging the 2021 drought. (They're so common now you have to date them.) The river wasn't in a generous mood, but we still managed to catch a few small brookies and I landed a grayling that made my day. The fish wasn't especially large, but grayling are native to the Big Hole and the river is now their last indigenous holdout in the state, so catching one is like finding an arrowhead.[51]

In the next to the last chapter of *All the Time in the World*, Gierach tells an angling adventure story that is representative of others he has told. He and his friend Vince travel by car over Rocky Mountain National Park's Trail Ridge Road. When they arrive at their fishing locale, a small stream, we learn it is one that Gierach had happily fished decades earlier. As per usual, Gierach does not divulge *exactly* where he has gone, but he lets you know they were after colorful brook trout no more than 10 inches long—his favorite species and size in his preferred water. How he fished we can well imagine—with light tackle, such as a seven-foot bamboo rod and an elk-hair caddis. Here is how he describes what happened:

> Vince and I warmed up as usual, cherry-picking easy spots with casually sloppy casts and then began to bear down as we picked out the less obvious honey holes. . . . I engineered a cast that dropped the fly in the quarter inch of bankside current that would draw it into the eddy for a single slow revolution. I managed to pull off a couple of good ones without getting a grab, but nonetheless a switch had been thrown; I was now taking the

51. Gierach, *All the Time in the World*, 203.

> creek on its own terms, fishing for its 9-inch brookies as if they each weighed 5 pounds.[52]

With Gierach's essays, we come to the end of this chapter, "Angling Adventure Essays," the 12th genre of fishing-fish-water literature described in this book. This chapter has been the longest because, perhaps every angler has a tale or two to share, and many of them have recorded their piscatorial experiences and reflections.

52. Gierach, *All the Time in the World*, 193.

Tail for the Tales

Diving Fish at Sunset

WITH THE LAST GENRE covered, we come to the end of *Gilgamesh to Gierach: 4000 Years of Fishing, Fish, and Water Stories.* Over 300 stories have been told, however briefly, drawn from almost as many books, articles, and other sources, including the Internet and films. Still, we only have sampled what relates to fish, fishing, and water from 2100 B.C.E. to 2024 C.E., from nursery rhymes to novels to philosophical ruminations. These samplings, I hope, will serve as teasers to entice the reader to get the complete and unabridged versions from the sources cited or to pick up one of the sources from one's own bookshelf and delve into the book again or for the first time.

May we never forget remarkable characters such as Homer's Odysseus; Aesop's monkeys; St. Brendan the Navigator; Jules Verne's harpooner, Ned Land; Hemingway's Santiago, the old man of the sea; Gus Orviston and his fisher-gal Eddy; Harry Middleton's Elias Wonder; Little Nemo; Bill Blossom, the poacher; pungent Mr. Snow; Norman Maclean's brother Paul; Gierach's pal A. K. Best; and many others in impressively crafted stories, true or well-imagined.

I recall these notable lines: from the Roman poet Martial: "Who has not seen the scarus rise, decoyed and caught by fraudful flies"; from the Christian Bible, Jesus saying, "Cast your net on the right side of the boat"; Izaak Walton offering us these sweet words: "O the Gallant fisher's life, it is the best of any! 'Tis full of pleasure, void of strife, and 'tis beloved by many"; from *Grimms' Fairy Tales*: "Flounder, flounder in the sea, Come, I pray thee, here to me"; W. B. Yeats gave us: "I went out to the hazel wood because a fire was in my head and cut and peeled a hazel wand . . . and caught a little silver trout"; Norman Maclean's "Eventually all things merge into one and a river runs through it . . . I am haunted by waters"; and, finally, John Gierach's "Just to be on the road is good in a deep American way, but to be on the road going fishing is almost too good for words."

As rich and meaningful as the above lines are, I add one more to them, prose from Robert Traver (pen name for John Voelker, former Michigan Supreme Court justice) in his book *Trout Madness*. With its 21 fly-fishing stories, the book is offered as "a dissertation on the symptoms and pathology of this incurable disease by one of its victims," the tales being "as true as can reasonably be expected of a fisherman"—or fisherwoman, he now might add. Below are Traver's excellent words on our sport. With them, I bring this book to a close.

> I fish because I love to. Because I love the environs where trout are found, which are invariably beautiful, and hate the environs where crowds of people are found, which are invariably ugly. . . . Because trout do not lie or cheat and cannot be bought or bribed, or impressed by power, but respond only to quietude and humility, and endless patience. Because I suspect that men are going this way for the last time and I for one don't want to waste the trip. . . . And finally, not because I regard fishing as being so terribly important, but because I suspect that so many of the other concerns of men are equally unimportant and not nearly so much fun.[1]

Thank you, your honor.

1. Robert Traver, aka John Voelker, *Anatomy of a Fisherman*, 10. Also, see *Trout Madness*, x, 113, and others that reflect similar words and sentiments.

Bibliography

"Aesop's Fables." Wikipedia. Last edited Apr 28, 2024. https://en.wikipedia.org/wiki/Aesop%27s_Fables#:~:text=Apollonius%20of%20Tyana%2C%20a%201st,or%20not%20to%20do%20it.

Berlin, Sven. *Jonah's Dream: A Meditation on Fishing.* Los Angeles: William Kaufmann, 1964.

Berners, Juliana. *Treatyse.* Translated by Alfred Duggan. *Sports Illustrated*, May 20, 1957. https://vault.si.com/vault/1957/05/20/the-treatise-of-fishing-with-an-angle.

Bethge, Gerry. "The Best Fishing Songs of All Time." OutdoorLife, Apr 20, 2021. https://www.outdoorlife.com/best-fishing-songs-all-time/.

Bishop, Elvin. "Fishin'." Genius. 1974. https://genius.com/Elvin-bishop-fishin-lyrics.

Boeckmann, Catherine. "Taller-Than-Typical Tales!" Last updated Aug 8, 2022. https://www.almanac.com/tall-tales-and-fish-stories.

Brautigan, Richard. *Trout Fishing in America, The Pill Versus the Springhill Disaster, and In Watermelon Sugar.* Boston: Houghton Mifflin/Seymour Laurence, 1968.

Brooke, Rupert. "Heaven." http://english.emory.edu/LostPoets/Heaven.html.

Brooks, Charles E. *Fishing Yellowstone Waters.* Piscataway, NJ: Winchester Press, 1984.

Brooks, Joe. *Trout Fishing.* New York: Harper and Row/Outdoor Life, 1972.

Brown, Margaret Wise. *The Fish With the Deep Sea Smile.* Bath, UK: Paragon Press, 2013.

Carter, Jimmy. *An Outdoor Journal: Adventures and Reflections.*

Cavoukian, Raffi. *Baby Beluga.* New York: Knopf Books for Young Readers, 1997.

Coleridge, Samuel Taylor. "Rime of the Ancient Mariner." In *The Literature of England: An Anthology and a History*, edited by George B. Woods et al., 2:433. Chicago: Scott, Foresman and Company, 1947.

Collodi, Carlo. *Pinocchio.* Translated by Geoffrey Brock. New York: New York Review of Books, 2009.

"Critical Essays Major Symbols in *Moby-Dick*." Cliffsnotes. https://www.cliffsnotes.com/literature/m/mobydick/critical-essays/major-symbols-in-mobydick.

Dahl, Roald. *Danny: The Champion of the World.* New York: Alfred A. Knopf, 1998.

de La Fontaine, Jean. "The Fishes and the Shepherd Who Played the Flute." Full Reads. https://fullreads.com/poetry/the-fishes-and-the-shepherd-who-played-the-flute/.

———. "The Little Fish and the Fisherman." https://e-libr.com/la-fontaine-the-little-fish-and-the-fisherman/.

DeMott, Robert, ed. *Astream: American Writers on Fly Fishing.* New York: Skyhorse Publishing, 2012.

Dodsley, Robert. *Select Fables of Esop and Other Fabulists.* Ann Arbor, MI: University of Michigan, 2009.

Dr. Seuss. *One Fish Two Fish Red Fish Blue Fish.* New York: Random House, 1988.

Duncan, David James. *The River Why.* Toronto: Bantam, 1983.

Dylan, Bob. "Boots of Spanish Leather." BobDylan.com, 1963. https://www.bobdylan.com/songs/boots-spanish-leather/.

Eiseley, Loren. *The Immense Journey.* New York: Random House, 1957.

Eliot, George. *Middlemarch.* New York: Penguin Classics, 1994.

"Finn MacCumhaill and the Salmon of Knowledge." Your Irish. https://www.yourirish.com/folklore/salmon-of-wisdom.

Folk-Lore and Fable: Aesop, Grimm, Andersen, With Introductions and Notes. New York: P. F. Collier and Son Corporation, 1937.

Gaba, Brett. "The Last American Steelheader in Terrace." *Steelheader's Journal* 7 (2021) 89–90.

Gabárain, Cesáreo. *"Tu has venido a la orilla"* ("You Have Come Down to the Lakeshore"). Translated by Madeleine Forell Marshall. 1976.

Gibbs Otis. "Big Whiskers—Otis Gibbs (Official Video)." YouTube, Apr 16, 2024. https://www.youtube.com/watch?v=lShDR_Husn4.

Gierach, John. *All the Time in the World.* New York: Simon and Schuster, 2023.

———. *Dances With Trout.* New York: Fireside, Simon and Schuster, 1994.

———. *Trout Bum.* Boulder, CO: Pruett Publishing, 1986.

———. *The View From Rat Lake: Essays on the Sport of Fly Fishing.* Boulder, CO: Pruett Publishing, 1988.

Godfrey, Ed. "The Best Fishing Songs Ever Recorded." *The Oklahoman*, Jul 19, 2020. https://www.oklahoman.com/story/sports/columns/2020/07/19/the-best-fishing-songs-ever-recorded/60391219007/.

Grahame, Kenneth. *The Wind in the Willows.*

Gray, Ed, ed. *Tales From Gray's: Selections From Gray's Sporting Journal, 1975–1985.* South Hampton, MA: GSJ Press, 1986.

Guest, Edgar. "A Boy and His Dad." Poets.org. https://poets.org/poem/boy-and-his-dad.

Guthrie, Woody. "The Crawdad Song." Genius. https://genius.com/Woody-guthrie-crawdad-song-lyrics.

———. "Talking Fishing Blues." WoodyGuthrie.org. 1961. https://www.woodyguthrie.org/Lyrics/Talking_Fishing_Blues.htm.

Haddawy, Husain, trans. *The Arabian Nights.* New York: W. W. Norton, 1990.

Haien, Jeannette. *The All of It.* New York: Harper Perennial, 1986.

Hammerstein, Oscar, II. "Mister Snow." RodgersandHamerstein.com. 1945. https://rodgersandhammerstein.com/song/carousel/mister-snow/.

Harman, Dianne. *Murder in Cuba.* CreateSpace, 2016.

Heaney, Seamus. *Electric Light.* New York: Farrar, Straus and Giroux, 2001.

Heavey, Bill. "Life on the Fly." *Wall Street Journal*, Mar 20, 2021.

Hemingway, Ernest. *The Old Man and the Sea.* New York: Scribner Paperback Fiction, 1995.

Heyward, DuBose, and Ira Gershwin. "Summertime." Genius. 1935. https://genius.com/George-gershwin-summertime-lyrics.

Hoffman, Al, and Norman Gimbel. "A Whale of a Tale." Disney.fandom. 1954. https://disney.fandom.com/wiki/A_Whale_of_a_Tale.

Homer. *The Odyssey.* Translated by A. S. Klein. https://www.perseus.tufts.edu/hopper/text?doc=Perseus%3Atext%3A1999.01.0136

———. *The Odyssey*. Translated by Robert Fitzgerald. New York: Farrar, Straus, and Giroux, 1998.

Hopkins, Gerard Manley. "Pied Beauty." Poetry Foundation. https://www.poetryfoundation.org/poems/44399/pied-beauty.

Hughes, Henry, ed. *The Art of Angling: Poems About Fishing*. Everyman's Library Pocket Poets. New York: Alfred A. Knopf, 2011.

Hunt, Leigh. "To a Fish/A Fish Answers." Poetry by Heart. https://www.poetrybyheart.org.uk/poems/to-a-fish-a-fish-answer.

Hurteau, Dave. "Jump In." *Field and Stream* (June–July 2019) 14.

Ibister, Danielle J., ed. *The Fly Fishing Anthology*. Stillwater, MN: Voyageur Press, 2004.

"The International Fishery of the 16th Century." Heritage: Newfoundland & Labrador. https://www.heritage.nf.ca/articles/exploration/16th-century-fishery.php.

Ives, Burl. "The Eddystone Light." Street Directory. https://www.streetdirectory.com/lyricadvisor/song/ulwee/the_eddystone_light/.

Jackson, Erik Forrest. *Fairy Tales From the Brothers Grimm*. New York: Penguin Workshop, 2018.

"John Gierach." Trout Unlimited. https://www.tu.org/gierach/.

Keen, Robert Earl. "The Five Pound Bass." Genius. 1989, https://genius.com/Robert-earl-keen-the-five-pound-bass-lyrics.

"Kevin of Glendalough." Orthodox Wiki. Last edited Jun 3, 2022. https://orthodoxwiki.org/Kevin_of_Glendalough.

Kilgannon, Corey. "Miracle? Dream? Prank? Fish Talks, Town Buzzes." *New York Times*, Mar 15, 2003.

Kipling, Rudyard. *Captains Courageous*. London: Penguin Books, 2005.

———. *Just So Stories for Children*. London: Macmillan, 1902.

Krebs, Natalie. "17 Hilarious Pat McManus Quotes About the Outdoors." OutdoorLife, Apr 20, 2021. https://www.outdoorlife.com/17-hilarious-pat-mcmanus-quotes-about-outdoors/.

Krivanec, Karel, et al. *Czech Nymph and Other Related Fly Fishing Methods*. Czech Republic: Grayling and Trout Publishing, 2008.

Kurlansky, Mark. *Cod: A Biography of the Fish That Changed the World*. New York: Penguin Books, 1997.

———. *The Unreasonable Virtue of Fly Fishing*. New York: Bloomsbury, 2019.

———. *The Unreasonable Virtue of Fly Fishing*. New York: Bloomsbury, 2021.

London, James. "The Man at the Nore." Folk Song and Music Hall. 1866. http://folksongandmusichall.com/index.php/man-at-the-nore-the.

Longfellow, Henry Wadsworth. "The Angler's Song." https://www.hwlongfellow.org/poems_poem.php?pid=2107.

"Los peces en el río" ("The Fish in the River"). Enforex. https://www.enforex.com/culture/peces-rio.html.

Lyons, Nick, ed. *The Gigantic Book of Fishing Stories*. New York: Skyhorse Publishing, 2007.

———. *Hemingway on Fishing*. New York: Lyons Press, 2000.

Macaulay, Rose. *The Towers of Trebizond*. New York: New York Review Books, 1956.

MacDonald, Margaret Read, and Brian W. Sturm. *The Storyteller's Sourcebook: A Subject, Title, and Motif Index to Folklore Collections for Children*. Detroit: Gale Group, 2001.

Maclean, Norman. *A River Runs Through It*. Chicago: University of Chicago, 1970.

Marks, Godfrey. "Sailing, Sailing." Bounding Main. 1880. http://boundingmain.com/music/lyrics/sailing-sailing/.

Marlowe, Christopher. "The Passionate Shepherd to His Love." https://www.poetryfoundation.org/poems/44675/the-passionate-shepherd-to-his-love.

Martialis, Marcus Valerius. *The Twelve Books of Epigrams*. London: George Routledge & Sons.

McCaughrean, Geraldine. *One Thousand and One Arabian Nights*. Oxford: Oxford University Press, 1982.

McGuane, Thomas. *The Longest Silence: A Life in Fishing*. New York: Vintage Books, 1999.

McKean, Andrew. "Go With the Flow on the Mo." *Game & Fish (West)* (June–July 2021) 67.

McManus, Patrick F. *They Shoot Canoes, Don't They?* New York: Henry Holt and Company, 1981.

Meisner, Randy, et al. "Take It to the Limit." Genius. 1975. https://genius.com/Eagles-take-it-to-the-limit-lyrics.

Melville, Herman. *Moby Dick*. Pleasantville, NY: Reader's Digest Association, 1980.

———. *Moby Dick*. Pleasantville, NY: Reader's Digest Association, 1989.

Middleton, Harry. *The Earth Is Enough: Growing Up in a World of Flyfishing, Trout, and Old Men*. New York: Simon and Schuster, 1989.

Morris, Holly, ed. *A Different Angle: Fly Fishing Stories by Women*. Seattle: Seal Press, 1995.

Muggeridge, Malcolm. "Swallows and Amazons Book Review, 1930." *The Manchester Guardian*, Jul 21, 1930. https://www.theguardian.com/books/from-the-archive-blog/2016/aug/20/swallows-and-amazons-review-1930-archive.

"Native American Legends." https://www.fs.usda.gov/Internet/FSE_DOCUMENTS/fsbdev2_025634.pdf.

Norton, Mary. *The Borrowers*.

O'Meara, John J. *The Voyage of St. Brendan the Navigator*. Dublin: Four Courts Press, 1994.

Opie, Iona, and Peter Opie, eds. *The Oxford Dictionary of Nursery Rhymes*. New York: Oxford University Press, 1997.

Ozaki, Y. T. *Japanese Fairy Tales*. New York: A. L. Burt, 1908.

Philbrick, Nathaniel. *In the Heart of the Sea: The Tragedy of the Whaleship Essex*.

Pindyck, Eben. "Ancient Carping." In *The Drake* 24.4 (Winter 2022–23) 32.

Pliny the Elder. *The Natural History*. Translated by H. Rackham et al. http://www.attalus.org/info/pliny_hn.html.

Ransome, Arthur. *Swallows and Amazons*. Boston: David R. Godine, 1985.

Rash, Ron. "Speckled Trout." Poetry Foundation. https://www.poetryfoundation.org/poems/46434/speckled-trout.

Redford, Robert, dir. *A River Runs Through It*. Film. Columbia Pictures, 1992.

Reid, Robert. "Fly Fishing Mysteries." http://www.castingintomystery.com/angling-arts/fly-fishing-mysteries/.

Rinehart, Mary Roberts. *Tenting To-Night*. Boston: Houghton Mifflin, 1918.

"Roderick Haig-Brown Quotes." AZ Quotes. https://www.azquotes.com/author/23817-Roderick_Haig_Brown.

Rundell, Joseph Benjamin, ed. *The Fables of Aesop*. New York: A. L. Burt, ~1900–1920.

Sandars, N. K., ed. *The Epic of Gilgamesh*. London: Penguin Books, 2006.

Schullery, Paul. *Cowboy Trout: Western Fly Fishing As If It Matters.* Helena, MT: Montana Historical Society, 2006.

Scott, Genio C. *Fishing in American Waters.* Secaucus, NJ: Castle Books, 1989.

Scott, Mike, and Steve Wickham. "Fisherman's Blues." Musixmatch. 1986. https://www.musixmatch.com/lyrics/The-Waterboys/Fisherman-s-Blues.

Shannon, David. *Jangles: A BIG Fish Story.* New York: Blue Sky Press, 2012.

Sloane, Everett. "The Fishin' Hole." Genius. 1961. https://genius.com/Andy-griffith-the-fishin-hole-lyrics.

Smith, Chris. "Fishin' Blues." Bluegrass Messengers. 1911. http://bluegrassmessengers.com/fishing-blues—henry-thomas-1928.aspx.

Sowder, Michael. "Fishing, His Birthday." Poetry Foundation. https://www.poetryfoundation.org/poems/53623/fishing-his-birthday.

"The Story of Urashima Tarō, the Fisher Lad." Lit2Go. https://etc.usf.edu/lit2go/72/japanese-fairy-tales/4881/the-story-of-urashima-taro-the-fisher-lad/.

Sugimoto, Chiyino. *Picture Tales From the Japanese.* New York: Frederick A. Stokepeople, 1923.

Swift, Jonathan. *Gulliver's Travels.*

The Complete Francis of Assisi: His Life, the Complete Writings, and the Little Flowers. Brewster, MA: Paraclete, 1989.

The Fables of Pilpay. London: E. Lumley, 1852.

Thoreau, Henry David. *The Maine Woods.* New Haven: Yale University, 2009.

———. *Walden.* https://commons.digitalthoreau.org/walden/.

———. *Walden and Civil Disobedience.* New York: New American Library, 1996.

Tosches, Rich. *Zipping My Fly: Moments in the Life of an American Sportsman.* New York: Berkley Publishing Group, 2002.

Traver, Robert. *Anatomy of a Fisherman.* Salt Lake City: Peregrine Smith, 1978.

———. *Trout Madness: Being a Dissertation of the Symptoms and Pathology of the Incurable Disease by One of Its Victims.* New York: St. Martin's, 1960.

Twain, Mark. *The Adventures of Tom Sawyer.* Hartford, CT: American Publishing, 1876.

Verne, Jules. *20,000 Leagues Under the Sea.* New York: Penguin Publishing, 2010.

Wallace, Daniel. *Big Fish: A Novel of Mythic Proportions.* Chapel Hill, NC: Algonquin Books, 1998.

Walton, Izaak. *The Compleat Angler.* Illustrated by Arthur Rackham. New York: Weathervane Books, 1931.

wayupstream1. "The Complete Angler—Full Length Version." YouTube, Jan 5, 2011. https://www.youtube.com/watch?v=1r2nRfnpWxw.

White, James W. *Fly-fishing the Arctic Circle to Tasmania: A Preacher's Adventures and Reflections.* Eugene, OR: Resource Publications, 2019.

———. "The Miraculous Draught of Fishes." *High Country Angler* (Winter 2021) 41.

———. *Round Boys Great Adventures.* Cincinnati, OH: Whitefish Press, 2010.

———. "Where the Big Fish Go . . . The Lower Gunnison River." *Fly Fisherman Magazine* 16.5 (July 1985) 44–45.

Whiting, William. "Eternal Father, Strong To Save." Hymnary. https://hymnary.org/text/eternal_father_strong_to_save_whose_arm.

Whitlock, Dave. "My Favorite Trout Experiences—#2, Nymphin' Deschutes Redbands." *Trout Magazine* (Summer 2021) 67–68.

"Who Was Dagon in the Bible?" Got Questions. https://www.gotquestions.org/who-Dagon.html.

Williams, Dar. "Fishing in the Morning." Street Directory, 2003. https://www.streetdirectory.com/lyricadvisor/song/acupa/fishing_in_the_morning/.

Williams, Hank. "Long Gone Lonesome Blues." Genius. 1950. https://genius.com/Hank-williams-long-gone-lonesome-blues-lyrics.

Wyss, Johann David. *Swiss Family Robinson.* https://www.gutenberg.org/files/11703/11703-h/11703-h.htm.

www.ingramcontent.com/pod-product-compliance
Lightning Source LLC
Chambersburg PA
CBHW070629310726
48982CB00001B/213
* 9 7 9 8 3 8 5 2 0 5 6 9 1 *